THE GOLDEN SEQUENCE

THE GOLDEN SEQUENCE

A Fourfold Study of the
Spiritual Life

BY

EVELYN UNDERHILL

FELLOW OF KING'S COLLEGE, LONDON

Wipf and Stock Publishers
150 West Broadway • Eugene OR 97401

Wipf and Stock Publishers
150 West Broadway
Eugene, Oregon 97401

The Golden Sequence
By Underhill, Evelyn
©1932 Wilkinson, R.D.
ISBN: 1-57910-952-7
Publication Date: April, 2002
Previously published by Methuen & Co. Ltd., 1932.

TO
LUCY MENZIES
WITH MUCH LOVE

PREFACE

THIS is a personal little book. Its aim is not the establishment of some new thesis. It merely represents the precipitation of my own thoughts, as they have moved to and fro during the last few years, along a line which has the spiritual doctrine of St. John of the Cross at one end, and the philosophy of Professor Whitehead at the other: though I fear that few traces of the influence of these august god-parents appear in the finished result. The book, then, does not pretend to completeness ; and is not to be regarded as a treatise, still less as a manual of the spiritual life. It consists of what ancient writers on these themes were accustomed to call ' considerations ' ; offered to those who share the writer's passion for the exploration of the realities, and interpretation of the experiences, which are signified by the familiar words and symbols of dogmatic religion.

I am sure that this passion—even where it takes the form of an exaggerated impatience of traditional language and practice—is on the whole a symptom of spiritual vitality ; and that its legitimate demands should be met, with candour and without nervousness, by those who adhere to Christian theism and believe its majestic declarations to be the best of all answers to the problem of human life. For although it is almost certainly an error, to speak of the 'modern soul' as though it were distinct in kind from all that have gone before, and had nothing to learn from its spiritual ancestors ; yet the great changes which have come with the present century, and especially the new proportion in which the universe is now seen by us, have deeply affected our attitude towards those realities which do not change. The ancient language of faith can no longer be taken for granted. Its terms must be re-examined, if their abiding significance is to be understood. And it is surely a work of piety to do this ; and bring back into currency these lovely tokens of our spiritual *Patria* and spiritual wealth.

For the times are crucial for the future of human religion. On one hand it tends more and more towards a shallow immanentism, an emphasis upon the here-and-now, which replaces adoration by altruism, and Charity by humanitarian sentiment. This pious naturalism abounds in good works ; but it lacks the creative energy which comes only from the eternal sources of power. On the other hand, the fresh acknowledgement of the Transcendent, the awe-struck sense of God, the prophetic insistence on the Holy, which distinguishes the work of Otto, Barth and Brunner, and their numerous disciples, has brought with it a crushing sense of helplessness ; of an unbridged gap between action and contemplation, between the human and the divine. It is the peculiar work of the Christian doctrine of the Spirit,

PREFACE ix

to fill this gap ; and weave together the temporal and eternal strands in our strange human experience of reality, without any declension from that deep acknowledgement of Transcendent Majesty, that sense of our creaturely status over against the Eternal, which is the very salt of religion.

The title of the book is that given by liturgic custom to the noblest of all Christian hymns, the *Veni Sancte Spiritus* ; well known in a somewhat pedestrian translation to users of our standard English hymn-books. For these studies began as an attempt to enter more deeply into its unfathomable meaning, give a wider, richer and more supple interpretation to the neglected doctrine which it declares, and bring its phrases into direct relation with the interior experiences of men. Though here and there my meditations may seem to wander far from their inspiring cause, to me its music has been always present ; and will, I hope, be heard by my readers too. The four sections into which the work has fallen, do represent in some sense the fourfold relation between the created spirit and that Spirit Increate : for they cover first the revelation of its reality and the movement of response which it incites in us, and then the two capital means without which our destiny as spiritual beings can never be fulfilled. Some who read these pages will certainly complain, because little is said about Fellowship and Service ; activities which nowadays are often regarded as the substance, instead of the symptoms, of a living Christianity. To these critics

THE GOLDEN SEQUENCE

I can only say, that the subject of the book is that essential life, out of which real fellowship and service must proceed; for these are not the essence but the expression of the spiritual life in man. The saints abound in fellowship and service, because they are abandoned to the Spirit, and see life in relation to God, instead of God in relation to life; and therefore seize with delight on every circumstance of life, as material for the expression of Charity. This resort to first principles, this surrender to the priority of Spirit, and the embodiment of our faith in such meek devotional practice and symbolic action as shall stimulate the transcendental sense: this, I believe, is the chief spiritual lack of the modern world.

The first and last sections of this book incorporate the substance of a few passages which have already appeared in a paper on 'God and Spirit' read before the Anglican Fellowship, and afterwards printed in *Theology*; and in an article on 'Prayer and the Divine Immanence' contributed to *The Expository Times*. This material has been revised and largely re-written for the purpose of the present work.

E. U.

Whitsuntide, 1932

CONTENTS

SPIRIT

		PAGE
I	WHAT IS SPIRIT?	1
II	GOD IS SPIRIT	8
III	SPIRIT AS POWER	14
IV	SPIRIT AS PERSON	21
V	THE REVELATION OF SPIRIT	32

SPIRITUAL LIFE

I	CREATED SPIRIT	45
II	MAN NATURAL AND SUPERNATURAL	53
III	CREATIVE SPIRIT	63
IV	LIFE FINITE AND INFINITE	70
V	THE GIFTS OF THE SPIRIT	78
VI	THE TWOFOLD LIFE	90

PURIFICATION

I	THE ESSENCE OF PURGATION	97
II	THE CLEANSING OF THE SENSES	107
III	THE CLEANSING OF THE INTELLECT	115
IV	MEMORY AND IMAGINATION	126
V	WILL AND LOVE	135

PRAYER

		PAGE
I	THE SPAN OF PRAYER	147
II	ADORATION	158
III	COMMUNION	168
IV	ACTION	178
V	CONCLUSION	191

The frontispiece is reproduced from a photograph by
Etienne Houvet, Chartres.

Veni, Sancte Spiritus,
Et emitte coelitus
Lucis tuae radium.

Veni, pater pauperum,
Veni, dator munerum,
Veni, lumen cordium.

Consolator optime,
Dulcis hospes animae,
Dulce refrigerium.

In labore requies,
In aestu temperies,
In fletu solatium.

O Lux beatissima,
Reple cordis intima
Tuorum fidelium.

Sine tuo numine,
Nihil est in homine,
Nihil est innoxium.

Lava quod est sordidum,
Riga quod est aridum,
Sana quod est saucium.

Flecte quod est rigidum,
Fove quod est frigidum,
Rege quod est devium.

Da tuis fidelibus,
In te confidentibus,
Sacrum septenarium.

Da virtutis meritum,
Da salutis exitum,
Da perenne gaudium.

THE GOLDEN SEQUENCE

SPIRIT

I

WHAT IS SPIRIT?

'SPIRIT' and 'spiritual' are words which are constantly used and easily taken for granted by all writers upon religion—more constantly and easily, perhaps, than any of the other terms in the mysterious currency of faith. Many who hesitate at the name of God, find no difficulty in assuming the existence of Spirit. Yet as a matter of fact, there are few terms in the vocabulary of religion of which the true character and value is so difficult to capture and define. This difficulty is not peculiar to the philosophic pietist, recommending 'absolute spiritual values' which are as elusive as vitamins, and equally essential to life. It is already present in those New Testament documents from which the Christian theology of spirit is derived. These documents say much of that which Spirit does and demands: little or nothing of that which Spirit is. They leave us still facing the question: what *is* Spirit? and the more we look at this question, the more we realize that we cannot answer it.

'Spirit'—a word admittedly symbolic, and more suggestive than precise—does stand for something which is veritably known by us, ' dimly yet vividly ' as Von Hügel says; something most real and fundamental to our human world, permeating all deep human experience, though always lying just beyond the range of conceptual thought. Our experience of this ' something ' may be slight and fleeting, or profound and transforming. But it is always the experience of a living reality; an unseen energy other than ourselves, and having in its own right a range of being and of significance unconditioned by the narrow human world. This reality is not, like sunlight, susceptible of analysis. Its character is never truly clear to the logical levels of the mind. It is, as the Victorines declared, ' beyond reason ' though not ' against reason '. It is known, therefore, more richly by intuition than it can ever be by intellect; and, for reasons which will afterwards appear, most richly and steadily by those who accept, in some way or degree, the special disciplines of the religious life. Indeed it seems that only a life which has been slowly cleansed by the penetrating action of much prayer, can develop at all fully that peculiar sensitiveness in which Spirit is truly known, even though never understood. All the works which really tell us something about it,

WHAT IS SPIRIT?

and rouse our dull souls to a sense of its reality, come from those whose lives have been re-ordered in this sense. Their writings, so quiet, nourishing and humble, stand in sharp contrast to the dry, assured, and superficial cleverness of those who pronounce upon 'spiritual experience' from without. All the studies of mystical psychology ever written will give us less information here than one encounter with a contemplative saint.

And this alone enlightens us as to the first character of the terms 'Spirit' and 'spiritual life'. Their reference is to a rich and concrete reality, a genuine existence which is only truly known by contact, and only fully known by self-mergence; that substantial Being we call eternal, by contrast with the time-series in which our natural lives are immersed. For it is the special function of prayer to turn the self away from the time-series, and towards the eternal order; away from the apparent, and towards the significant; away from succession, and towards adoration and adherence. Prayer opens the doors of the psyche to the invasion of another order, which shall at its full term transform the very quality of our existence. And Spirit, in its most general sense, is our name for that world, life, Being, which is then apprehended by us; and for that quality in ourselves which is capable of such apprehension and response. Moreover, this sacred category, lying behind the native land of the intelligence, is not to be thought of lightly, vaguely, or coldly, as mere material for academic speculation.

We do not mean by it some tenuous region or plane of being to which physical considerations cannot apply. The whole witness of religion suggests that it is alive with an awful splendour, a range of personal action, which extends from the most tender and intimate workings on the individual soul, to the inconceivable energies and secret movements which can sometimes be detected behind the pageant of the visible world.

For all this, we must acknowledge that the word ' Spirit '—even though it carries the suggestions of an invisible and unbounded energy, a wind blowing where it listeth, a breath and life—is far too vague and general to be adequate. It is allusive not descriptive ; and will never convey to those who have not known them, the vivid realities of our supersensual experience. When we look back into its origins—the strange word *Ruach* of the Old Testament, the *Pneuma* of the New—we realize that these terms stand for man's fundamental but ineffable consciousness of the Unearthly ; and that the symbols which he uses to convey that consciousness derive their value, not from any true approximation to the experience—which always slips through the meshes of the mind—but from the fact that they have become charged with a certain quality of suggestion which can stir our latent sense of ' otherness '. They are essentially musical and poetic ; crystallize the intuition of an unseen Somewhat, unspeakable in its transcendence, yet giving all its significance to the activities of the seen.

WHAT IS SPIRIT?

As Otto has pointed out, this knowledge of Spirit is still tentative and unformed in the Old Testament. The alternate movements of love and fear which stir those sensitive to its pressure have something of the august simplicity of primitive art. Its transforming, saving, 'supernaturalizing' character, the immense possibilities that wait on its invasion of human life, are not yet understood: still less its metaphysical implications. It is known only in the rare and vivid experiences of the prophetic consciousness—those strange calls and overwhelming intuitions, in which the soul becomes aware of the presence and direct demand of God-Spirit. Yet even these embryonic perceptions of a living and acting Reality already turn the mind to a mysterious region, entirely transcending us yet intimately present with and through us. They assert the presence of a world and an energetic power over against us; the scene of secret experience, the spring of secret action, and—as we grow up in that world and that action—the occasion of great suffering and great joy.

This, and much more, is involved and suggested by the strange word 'Spirit'; even as used in the most general sense. And within this general sense it gives us, as we explore it, many grades and depths of reality; not easily to be harmonized within our limited span. At one end of the scale, it points with awe towards the nature of Absolute Being; in so far as Absolute Being is apprehended by us. 'God *is* Spirit.' At the other end, it is our best word for a certain fundamental essence or quality we divine in ourselves, the ground of our being, wherein our reality consists : a quality which confers on us a certain kinship with Absolute Being, and gives us a ' capacity for God '. This element of our many-levelled and unstable nature, emerging and becoming dominant, can transform us : ' that which is born of the Spirit, is spirit.'

Thus, whether we look at it from the objective or subjective point of view, this word Spirit is our label for the fundamental religious category. It stands for all we know or suspect of the supersensual, the non-successive ; and the range of experience and belief lying between its two extremes, divine and human, is the field not only of theology but of all personal religion. And as we mature and life becomes more transparent to us—at least in hours of recollection and peace—we find here the source of those mysterious movements, those hidden currents, by which human destinies are controlled. Yet even so this term ' Spirit ' alone is not enough for religion ; though it may easily be enough for philosophy. For religion is concerned, not merely with the non-extended and the supersensuous, but with the Holy. We may be sure that vast regions of existence lie beyond our sensory range ; and that the world invisible includes grades and kinds of being of which we are unable to conceive. But religion as such is not concerned with the totality of the mysterious. It loses its character and squanders its strength, when it leaves the strait way to

WHAT IS SPIRIT? 7

God for these by-path meadows. Its business is only with the Holy ; with the relationship between man, the derived, imperfect and embodied spirit, and the perfect, spaceless Spirit of all spirits—God. It affirms His living sanctity, His individual action, His overwhelming attraction and demand: and the nothingness of the soul, at least as regards its upward reaches, without that action—its fulfilment in the response to that attraction and demand. Therefore any attempt to study the ' spiritual life ' of man must begin here ; with the fluid concept under which he tries to express what he knows of the peculiar quality of that life, and its relation to its source and goal.

II

GOD IS SPIRIT

TWO of the names of God which are most characteristic of the New Testament seem—when we take them together and examine them closely—to contain or involve an almost complete doctrine of Spirit in its relation to the life of man. First, there is that absolute statement which the Fourth Gospel attributes to Christ Himself—' God *is* Spirit '; and the whole conception of the Divine nature which is implied by it. Next there is the term most commonly used by Him, and repeated by the Synoptists—' our Heavenly Father '. This of course is nearly always distorted by pious minds; which stress the protective, cherishing, humanistic note, and so blur the overwhelming supernatural affirmation. Yet it is only in the double declaration that our best name for the ultimate Reality is Spirit, and that nevertheless this same ineffable and wholly supernatural Spirit is father of our half-real souls, that we can hint the real mystery of our situation. Here, we do stand beyond the time-series, and declare our own deepest being to be rooted in Eternal Life, to consist in a direct relationship with Reality. ' Unto

GOD IS SPIRIT

the rapting Spirit the rapt spright!' exclaimed Fotherby, enclosing our beatitude in a matchless phrase.

Neither of these expressions, of course, is peculiar to Christianity. All that they mean is already implied in the Psalms and the Prophets, and emerges in the deepest experiences of first-hand religion wherever found. But each receives in Christianity a new expansion and richness of content. The first term, 'God is Spirit', lifts us far beyond that world of succession which is the normal object of our consciousness, and gives precision to our deep sense of transcendent and abiding Reality. It clears away the spatial images which dog and blur religious thought, and places us in a world wholly other than the dimensional world of sense, and yet a world that is most truly here. It names, though it cannot describe, the Object of our metaphysical thirst. It endorses the instinctive upward glance of awakened souls : the strange awe and delight which falls upon these souls when they taste in moments of tranquillity that 'supreme Being, supreme Life, in Whom are all moments of time' and realize that looking up is the same as looking in, since beyond and within process, and alone giving meaning to process, is not merely Mind but that super-essential Life of which Mind is but one facet—the irresistible attraction of God-Spirit. Baron von Hügel tells us how in earliest childhood, before the moral struggle began, he felt all nature to 'be penetrated and saturated by a Spirit distinct from what I saw, distinct from myself the seer'—that inborn sense of God which is the ground-stuff of natural religion— and moreover that the essence of this purely religious joy consisted ' precisely in the fact that, beautiful as the external nature was, God did not consist even in its full totality, but was a Life, an Intelligence, a Love distinct from it all, in spite of His close penetration of it all '. Here then we seem to have the report of a primary experience of the Spirit, as known by an innate though still unformed genius for religion. And we see already in this naïve intuition the sharp withdrawal of the genuine religious sense from any merely immanental apprehension of God-Spirit; its emphasis on the distinctness of the divine. God is here a concrete Reality underlying all lesser realities; moulding, inspiring, and supporting His creation in every detail and at every point.

We can trace this apprehension of Spirit, in various degrees of richness and distinctness, right through human experience, from the child to the saint. Thus it is wonderfully given by Plotinus, in a passage which seems to anticipate the deepest intuitions of the Christian contemplatives. 'We must not', he says, 'think of ourselves as cut off from the source of Life; rather we breathe and consist in It, for It does not give Itself to us and then withdraw Itself, but *ever* lifts and bears us.' So too St. Hildegard hears the Spirit say : ' I am that living and fiery Essence of the divine substance that glows in the beauty of the fields. I shine in the

GOD IS SPIRIT

water, I burn in the sun, and the moon, and the stars, Mine is the mysterious force of the invisible wind . . . I permeate all things, that they may not die. I am Life.' And Angela of Foligno tells us how she saw in vision the whole universe spread before her; the ocean, and the abyss of space in which the world lies, and all things that exist therein. And in all this she could see nothing but the power and presence of God, in a way that she had no words to express; so that she cried out in her amazement: 'The whole world is impregnated with God!' And again Julian of Norwich, more homely in expression but not less profound, 'We are all in Him enclosed and He is enclosed in us!'

So 'God is Spirit' guarantees religion both in its most transcendental and its most penetrating aspects: in its certitude of Presence and of purpose; in its passionate desire for purification, its incurable 'otherness', its tendency towards the simple, the universal, the spaceless, which is yet the rich, the concrete, the Here. 'The Holy Spirit', says St. Thomas Aquinas, 'is God Himself as He is everywhere at all times'; and the very heart of all personal religion is the tendency of the created spirit to union with that Spirit-God. Thus the fact that our awareness of this Holy Spirit is so limited, fluctuating and sporadic, our understanding so coloured by apparent contradiction, is seen to be comparatively unimportant. The emphasis lies on God, the Fact of all Facts, and His penetrating action; not on the partial experiences of our uneven, tentative and many-levelled consciousness, still so uncertain in its grasp of all that lies beyond the world of sense.

For the doctrine of the Holy Spirit means that we acknowledge and adore the everywhere-present pressure of God; not only as a peculiar religious experience, not as a grace or influence sent out from another world or order, but as a personal holy Presence and Energy, the Lord and Giver of Life—in this world and yet distinct from it, penetrating all, yet other than all, the decisive factor in every situation. It means God entering into, working on and using the whole world of things, events, and persons; operating at various levels, and most deeply and freely in that world of souls where His creation shows a certain kinship with Himself.

> Veni, Sancte Spiritus,
> Et emitte coelitus
> Lucis tuae radium.

And this Presence is moulding, helping and pressing all His creation—on every plane, in every person, at every point—by the direct action of His divine influence, to move towards greater perfection, get nearer the pattern of His shining thought. That influence may be felt as the gentle pressure on which piety prefers to dwell, or as the shattering invasion of a compelling and purifying power. 'Mine', said the Voice to St. Hildegard, 'is the blast of the thundered word by which all things were made.' When we meditate on all this, we get a

GOD IS SPIRIT

wonderful sense of the unmeasured action of God, and the links that bind together the mysterious rhythms of nature, the great movements of history, and the hidden springs of Providence and prayer. ' The Divine will ', says Caussade, ' unites itself to our souls by a thousand different means ; and that which it adopts for us is always the best for us.'

Moreover, the fact of this holy spaceless Presence guarantees and informs all those graded, varied, contrasting self-disclosures of God, which together constitute the history of human religion ; and all those intimations of Eternity, those hints of an imperishable beauty, given to us through rifts in the natural scene. Our limited minds refuse to combine the ideas of the personal and the universal. We set them in opposition ; but that is almost certainly a mistake. The self-revelation of Spirit to its sense-conditioned creatures goes all the way from the cosmic to the homely. It can bless the votive candle, and burn in the star. Yet even so, the most awe-struck vision, the most humble communion, do but touch single strands on the fringed robe of this Reality who is both Will and Love. For Spirit, thus conceived, is God, the Pure Absolute, acting. And it is the prerogative of religion to discover this action informing every small event of our inward and outward existence : and thus give significance to the bewildering mesh of circumstance which hems us in, whilst leaving in untouched majesty that Abyss of Being which enfolds and transcends our island universe of faith.

III

SPIRIT AS POWER

SO wide and elastic a doctrine of Spirit as that which seems to emerge from these considerations is congenial enough to modern minds; which love to sweep a large area of experience and thought within the hospitable frontiers of a single definition, and are more concerned with breadth than depth. But if we left the matter here, unbalanced by its completing opposite, we should fail to account for all the most profound and most subtle experiences of men. There is little to distinguish such a conception of the Spirit from a general doctrine of the immanence of God; and this easy and deceptive simplification would slur for us some of the most significant and necessary outlines drawn by religion. Those who give it unconditioned adherence are already setting their faces towards quietism, and away from the energy of adoration: towards pantheism, and away from the awful distinctness of God.

Certainly we may speak, as the mystics often do, of the Ocean of God-Spirit: that 'Sea Pacific' of the Divine, bathing and penetrating all life, in which the soul in certain states seems to be sunk,

SPIRIT AS POWER

losing all separate action in those peaceful and powerful tides. But so doing we must keep steadily in mind the fact that this image merely describes one aspect, one phase—most deep and true indeed, yet not perhaps the most important for us—in our rich but never perfect experience of an infinite Reality that transcends the totality of our experiences, conceptions and beliefs. The most marked character of all Biblical references to the Spirit is by no means the sense of an unbounded Life ' in whom we live and move and have our being '—a conception, of course, which is taken from a Pagan source. It is true that the Divine Action fills the universe and that the most free and vigorous of created spirits is but a darting shrimp in that unsounded sea. But the great Biblical writers owe their power to the fact that they knew deeper levels of spiritual experience than this. The compensating revelations of a terrible holiness and a profound tenderness, which gradually emerge in the Old Testament and are fully declared in the New, require as their background something very different from a merely immanental religious philosophy. For the men of the Bible the Spirit is never fully here ; a calm, enveloping Presence like the Plotinian *psyche*, penetrating the human world. Their emphasis is on its distinctness.

Veni, Sancte Spiritus

It is wholly other ; the **Object, not of philosophic** speculation, but of direct and awe-struck experience.

We are here in the presence of that fundamental dualism, which lies at the very heart of human religion.

To 'receive the Spirit' then, is not merely to open our eyes or even our souls on our real situation, penetrated and sustained as we are by the Being of God. It means a fresh situation, in which the first movement comes from the hidden world over against us; the passive reception of a more abundant life, which is never to be won by the creature's deliberate efforts; the prophetic 'gift' of Spirit; the crucial Pauline change from *psyche* to *pneuma*. Mild notions of a general immanence of Spirit must give way before that awe-struck sense of imminence which is the characteristic note of the Biblical doctrine of God. There is constantly implied in the religious outlook of the Old and New Testament writers, the expected invasion of another order over against the historical and human. Here, Spirit always represents the unconditioned action, the awful intervention of the very Life of God; at once a living spring and a devouring fire. The world of the Bible is not wholly built up by the quiet action of aqueous deposits. Its various structure witnesses to volcanic periods; when another order intervenes, with power to compel and transform.

'The Holy Spirit shall come on thee and the power of the most High overshadow thee. . . . Elizabeth was filled with the Holy Spirit . . . He shall baptize you with the Holy Spirit. . . . Jesus returned in the power of the Spirit. . . . Unto him

SPIRIT AS POWER 17

that blasphemeth against the Holy Spirit it shall not be forgiven. . . . He breathed on them and said, Receive ye the Holy Spirit. . . . Ye shall receive power after that the Holy Spirit is come upon you. . . . As I began to speak, the Holy Spirit fell on them. . . . Christ, through the eternal Spirit, offered himself without spot to God. . . . Resist not the Spirit. . . . Ye are sealed unto the Holy Spirit. . . . An habitation of God through the Spirit . . . where the Spirit of the Lord is, there is liberty.'

These texts, taken almost at random from the countless references of the New Testament, do give us when we strip them of pietistic associations, an overwhelming sense of vigorous and incalculable action ; an Energy that intervenes, breaks through from another plane of being, to modify or transform the chain of cause and effect. As we dwell on them, we receive the strong impression of one order acting on and through another order : of the whole human scene as subject to the free and mysterious action of a Creative Power. This sense of an imminent Act reaches its full intensity, and is expressed with poetic energy, in the prophetic and apocalyptic writers ; but it is essential to all living Christianity. The life of prayer hinges on it. It underlies all sacramental religion.

> Veni, Sancte Spiritus,
> Et emitte coelitus
> Lucis tuae radium.

18 THE GOLDEN SEQUENCE

The Church's great hymn to the Spirit, the Golden Sequence, beginning with the word *Come*, presents the very essence of Biblical religion ; and marks the line of cleavage between natural and supernatural theology.

For when the Spirit is defined in the Christian Creed, not only as Lord and Giver of Life, but as One who 'spake by the Prophets', the Church takes her departure from any doctrine which merely equates the Holy Spirit with the general immanence of God. Here, we are asked to acknowledge the free and personal action of the Absolute on and through individuals : using, modifying, or even thwarting the stream of causation we know as Natural Law. We are invited to recognize that action working within history, sometimes gradually, but sometimes suddenly ; bringing forth prophets, saints, men of action ; compelling them in defiance of all natural prudence to declare the Divine Will, do the Divine Work. In the controlling and enlightening Paraclete promised in the Fourth Gospel, who is the real hero of the Book of Acts, we experience the working of that same Spirit who rules the pageant of the heavens and sways the tides of history : here proceeding from the Heart of Deity to overrule and energize the clumsy efforts of imperfect men. Here we find a place for all those strange episodes in history where we feel another order intervening, and the march of events seems to pass beyond human control. So too those moments when everything seems to hang on the appearance

SPIRIT AS POWER

of a particular person, leader, reformer or saint; or, yet more confounding, the crucial part which some very simple and apparently unsuitable person is abruptly called to play—these receive a certain explanation, even though the implied facts exceed anything we are able to comprehend. For here, all that we know of the action of personality—even in its poor human expression—requires us to infer its influence on the mysterious currents that control the great and little histories of the world.

'O Action Divine!' cries Caussade, 'you have unveiled to me your immensity. I can make no step save within your unmeasured Heart. All which flows from you to-day, flowed yesterday. Your abyss is the bed of that river of graces which pours forth without ceasing—all is upheld and all is moved by you. Therefore I need seek you no more within the narrow limits of a book, of the life of a Saint, of a sublime idea. These are mere drops from that Ocean which I see poured out on all creation. The Divine Action overwhelms them all. They are but atoms which disappear within that abyss.'

Here the general sense of God Immanent, penetrating and supporting His creation, is completed by the sense of God Acting, and wholly present in the act. And this free and loving action is sometimes perceived by us operating over a wide span; sometimes in astonishing detail and intensity within a single soul. Both must be held together, in defiance of consistency, if we are to express the rich paradox of Spirit as self-revealed to men. Again and again naturalism strays from this, the only religious attitude ; and again and again our view of reality suffers a corresponding impoverishment.

IV

SPIRIT AS PERSON

THE mind which has reached this point in its exploration of the strange word Spirit, may well feel baffled by the paradox which confronts it. For how shall the 'tranquil operations of perpetual Providence' be reconciled with those abrupt experiences of an invading Life and Power, of personal and incalculable contacts, which are never wholly absent from the religious intuitions of great souls? Yet it is certain that these contrasting experiences of a Reality that is one—of that Spirit which, as St. Thomas says, 'both brings God to the soul and places the soul in God '—form the warp and weft of a full religious life. Though we must acknowledge a perfect continuity between that Creative Spirit disclosed by the physical universe and the Holy Spirit of Divine Love, yet here we reach an experience which is wholly 'other' and for which no degree of nature-mysticism can prepare the soul. Life, as that soul's awareness deepens, is more and more known to be immersed in and penetrated by a living spiritual order. But it is also known to be subject to sudden new incitements, fresh personal lights and calls and penetrations, the ceaseless possibility of novelty; as that same abiding spiritual order floods and works upon the stuff of our successive life. It is true that the world is already 'pregnant with God'; yet also true that the key-word of our spiritual life is 'Come'. The 'Power of the Spirit' is no inborn possession of the creature. There is no place where God is not, no situation in which He is not there first; yet something from another dimension called the child Samuel, broke in upon the young Isaiah in the Temple, and on Saul on the Damascus road.

And here, that other name of God which is of all the most surely guaranteed by Christ's own experience and teaching—'our Heavenly Father'—comes with its rich suggestions of a personal action which is the outcome of a personal relationship, to qualify that sense of boundless Spirit which is the ground of natural religion. For this term carries us beyond the awed sense of an unmeasured Reality that is 'wholly other'; even beyond the confident belief in a creative and fostering Presence, as the origin of 'all that is'. It hints at a closer link, a certain profound likeness in nature, a fetter of love, between the 'rapting Spirit and rapt spright'. It sets up a relationship within which gifts and illuminations, genuine expansions and enrichments of our small experience, can be conceived as coming to the sense-conditioned creature from the free and generous action of a spaceless creative Power within the soul.

SPIRIT AS PERSON

Veni, pater pauperum,
Veni, dator munerum,
Veni, lumen cordium.

Religion is penetrated through and through by this conviction of human incompleteness; of our dependence on a personal Reality, which can and does make good the insufficiencies of a creature that emerges from the animal yet possesses a capacity for God. The Christian liturgy returns again and again to the thought of something given, sent, poured in from the Transcendent, and makes each sacrament the occasion of a heavenly gift. *Rorate coeli desuper! Pour* into our hearts love towards Thee! And though we may surely refer that sense of invasion, even of a shattering impact, which is a character of great transforming moments, to the narrow span of our space-conditioned consciousness; yet this too has its value, in so far as it maintains our sense of dependence on a present yet infinite Power.

So here we turn back from the contemplation of the Mystery of Being to our own situation, which is not less mysterious; our dimly-guessed and yet direct relationship with that unseen, all-penetrating Reality. 'The Spirit itself beareth witness with our spirit, that we are the children of God.' Now we begin to consider those elements in our own nature, for which the temporal order cannot account; and which, because of their subtlety and uneven manifestation, we easily push aside and neglect. And first we perceive that our curious power of standing away from succession and judging it to be incomplete,—that sense of the whole temporal world as dust and ashes, which is a phase in nearly every full awakening to God,—is a part of this witness to our mysterious kinship with the Unchanging. Though we arise within the time-series and are conditioned by it, we know by these signs that we have another citizenship; beyond succession, in the eternal order. Our small created spirits originate with God the Pure Spirit; owe their being to Him, and depend utterly on Him. Were this not so, the human soul could never have reached that realistic experience of the Spirit, which is characteristic of a fully expanded religious sense. God, Who is Absolute Being, is also the Father, Fount, and Origin of souls.

Nor do we mean by such an image to present our relation with Spirit as the relation of a finite something 'here', with an infinite Power 'there' which is yet utterly outside the world; but rather as an unbroken continuity, in the soul's essential ground, between the creature and the absolute creative Love. 'We are all in Himself enclosed', says Julian of Norwich, 'and He is enclosed in us.' In that filial adherence, even though it never rise to consciousness, we can find an explanation at once spiritual and reasonable for those direct movements and incitements of the soul—whether felt as steady pressure or as abrupt invasions—which are of the very substance of personal religion; so too those painful purifications by which, once it is awakened,

SPIRIT AS PERSON

it is pressed to establish harmony with the indwelling Power. 'The Spirit', says Caussade, 'keeps school within us, in the soul's ground. He listens and speaks, teaches, moves, turns and moulds it as He wills. Of these workings of Spirit on spirit, the person concerned knows as it seems almost nothing; yet comes from them with certain impressions by which he is completely renewed.' And the same essential truth—which is indeed the philosophic sanction of all incarnational and sacramental religion—is given in other terms by Von Hügel: 'The central conviction and doctrine of Christianity is the real prevenience and condescension of the real God—the penetration of spirit into sense, of the spaceless into space, of the Eternal into time, of God into man.' Here is a doctrine of the universe which already contains in germ a doctrine of redemption, and a life-history of the human soul. Prophecy and sanctity, Pentecost and Church, can all be resumed under this law; and not these alone, but all intimations of Holiness reaching us through finite things. These are partial exhibitions of one Divine method and act.

Thus we reach a truth of the transcendental order which, once accepted, must transform and control our whole attitude to the natural order. For it means first that we, knowers and beholders of that natural order, cannot fulfil our lives by a correspondence, however perfect, with the natural alone. Nor are we to be explained on evolutionary lines, as merely growing up from within it. 'Spirit' in its unearthly beauty, its overwhelming demand, breaks in from another world, which is over against us and yet within us ; to possess, purge and transform. And only under its penetrating action and through its indwelling presence can any human life become complete. Moreover, this penetrating action of God takes place, above all, through and in human spirits ; and along the paths of the common life. Here is the only territory known to us, in which nature and supernature meet and merge.

'Spirit and spirit, God and the creature', says Von Hügel again, 'are not two material bodies, of which one can only be where the other is not ; but, on the contrary, as regards our own spirit, God's Spirit ever works in closest penetration and stimulation of our own ; just as, in return, we cannot find God's Spirit simply separate from our own spirit within ourselves. Our spirit clothes and expresses His ; His Spirit first creates and then sustains and stimulates our own.'

It may well be that on this doctrine of the interpenetration of realities, the practical theology of the future will be built. Nor is it to be suspected as a disguised pantheism. No theologian of the modern world has been more consistent and emphatic than Von Hügel in his warnings concerning the impoverishment and perversion of the religious sense which comes from opening the door to any kind of pantheistic monism. These words are the words of a teacher intensely concerned to safeguard those twin truths of the eternal distinctness of God

SPIRIT AS PERSON 27

and the derivative being of man, without which we can never hope to construct a sane and realistic, because humble and creaturely, theology of the Spirit.

The pendulum swing of religious experience and religious thought has tended sometimes to overstress one, and sometimes the other, of these twin truths. Sometimes it is God's utter distinctness which is overwhelmingly felt ; as when Karl Barth exclaims that He stands ' over against man and all that is human, nowhere and never identical with that which *we* call God—the unconditioned Halt as against all human action, and the unconditioned Action as against all human rest '. This profound religious intuition, if taken alone, must land us in virtual or actual Deism ; and sterilizes the germ-cells of the spiritual life. Sometimes, on the other hand, it is God's immanence in, and total possession of, the soul which is most actual to us ; and this, unbalanced by its completing opposite, prepares the way for that pantheism which ever lies in wait for the exclusive mystic. Only the Christian theology of the Holy Spirit seems able to safeguard the deep truths in both these extremes, and by carrying them up to a higher synthesis, to create a landscape wide enough and rich enough for all the varied experiences of the spiritual life. The solemn awe with which we abase ourselves before the *numen* is here softened and humanized by the humble and loving response of human nature in its totality to the Divine Nature incarnate in Christ, and there disclosing on the narrow stage of history the ultimate mystery of redeeming love. And this outward gaze of faith is saved from a mere hopeless contemplation of the Other and the Perfect by the veritable experience of a Spirit of Love and Will already working ' in closest penetration and stimulation of our own ' ; a source of energy, and also a personal influence. So here we have three experiences or revelations of God-Spirit, each compensating and enriching the rest. And while every Godward tending soul will perhaps combine them in a different manner, and for none will their outlines be quite clear and neat, there is no healthy life of the spirit in which some response to each facet of this threefold revelation is not found.

So by the Christian doctrine of the Spirit we mean God Himself in His holy reality and love, in so far as these can be known to us : the utter distinctness of His Eternal Being, yet His intimate cherishing care for His whole creation. We do not mean some immaterial energy, the soul of an evolving universe. We mean a substantial Reality, which is there first in its absolute perfection and living plenitude ; which transcends yet penetrates our world, our activity, our souls, and draws its transforming power from the fact that it is already perfect. ' Holy ' Spirit, transcendent and dynamic, is at once other than our own spirits, other than the ' spirit of nature ' ; yet felt and known, in its ecstasy of divine generosity, in all the splendours of creation. And because truly living, personal, free, it is most

SPIRIT AS PERSON

sharply and personally known, most deeply operative, in the secret intercourse and discipline of the interior life of man. That Spirit infinitely exceeds while it informs the created; not merely in degree, but also in kind. Even the most feeble and fleeting religious experience is enough to assure us of that. It is not subject to the conditions of the striving evolutionary process, but free and distinct; and therefore able to intervene, pour out dowers of life and light, and reveal actual but unguessed levels of reality beyond the finite structure of the natural world.

Thus the twin names of 'Spirit' and 'Heavenly Father' do give us a sort of picture, imperfect but suggestive, of a Reality which satisfies our metaphysical cravings and is known in the fundamental experience of praying souls. First, the certitude of a most rich and living Fact, yet quite invisible and unearthly; a region of Spirit truly here, and already found in our first steps over the threshold of the sensible, yet stretching away to the unsearchable depths of the Divine life. And next, the penetrating and cherishing character of that World and Presence; so that the impact of its life upon us is also the impact of its love. This double sense of God—so near and all-penetrating, so steady in His pressure of the soul towards generosity, purity, nobleness, and yet so far away in His achieved perfection of that same generosity, purity and nobleness—this is the very heart of human religion. And as we hold these two facts together in meditation—that boundless Reality, in its delightfulness and wonder, this intimate, heart-piercing care—our own world shrinks, the world of daily life and even the greater world of religion ; and we know that it only has significance as the theatre of that ceaseless and many-levelled Divine Act. Then, penetrating all those finite facts, both physical and psychological, which make up the environment and conditioning character of our life, we know an Infinite Fact, personal and creative, whose moulding pressure and demands reach us through and in that finite environment to which our natural lives are tuned. For if the lovely natural scene is like a great fresco where we see the breadth and splendour of the thought of God, the soul is like a little bit of ivory, on which the same Artist works with an intimate and detailed love.

Such a doctrine of the holy, living Spirit's moulding action can never be translated into the terms of ' emergent evolution ' or other process : because it is of the essence of Christian philosophy, endorsed by Christian experience, to hold that Spirit is there first. ' With thee is the well of life '—the prime originating cause. Therefore, while Christian philosophy can in a general sense accept and spiritualize the evolutionary account of natural process, it cannot accept as complete the evolutionary account of cause. Beyond and within the natural, it requires the supernatural ; if all that has been revealed to it is to be expressed. And even the wholly natural, seen in spiritual regard, reveals in ever-deepening

SPIRIT AS PERSON

degrees a quality which points beyond itself. Thus Gerard Hopkins:

' The World is charged with the grandeur of God.
   It will flame out, like shining from shook foil;
   It gathers to a greatness, like the ooze of oil
Crushed . . .
            . . . Nature is never spent;
   There lives the dearest freshness deep down things;
And though the last lights off the black West went
   Oh, morning, at the brown brink eastward, springs—
Because the Holy Ghost over the bent
   World broods with warm breast and with ah! bright
      wings.'

The warm breast, fount of creative and cherishing life, is turned earthwards: the bright wings, spread out upon another, a transcendent, free, and perfect order of existence, reflect the radiance of Eternity. Surely a wonderful image of the Divine double action, and the Divine double love.

V

THE REVELATION OF SPIRIT

IF the first term of our inquiry, ' God is Spirit ', requires of us the most awestruck and unearthly conception of God, and opens the door to the fullest supernaturalism, the second term, ' Heavenly Father ', is found to bring Spirit within reach of sense ; the spaceless into space. It qualifies the dreadful vision of the numinous by the soul's own experience of intimate dependence on a creative and cherishing power. It guarantees the inexhaustibly deep and mysterious doctrines of Providence and Divine Love—those dearest treasures of faith. It opens the door alike to mystical and to sacramental religion : the humble self-giving of God Present along the tortuous paths of the created mind, and through the consecration of homely created things.

' It is clear ', says St. John of the Cross, ' that God, in order to set a soul in movement, and raise it from one extreme, the abjection of the creature, to the opposite extreme, that is to the infinite height of the divine union, must act gradually, gently, and in accordance with the nature of the soul. Now the ordinary mode of knowledge proper to the soul requires the use of the forms and images of created

THE REVELATION OF SPIRIT 33

things ; for we can know and savour nothing without the stimulation of the senses. Hence God, to raise the soul to supreme knowledge and do it with gentleness, must begin to touch her in her lowest extremity, that of the senses, in order to raise her gradually and in accordance with her proper nature to her other extremity—that spiritual wisdom which is independent of the senses. . . . God works man's perfection according to man's nature. He begins with that which is lowest and most external, and ends with that which is highest and most interior.'

In this great passage St. John is speaking of a far richer, more precise and more penetrating disclosure of Spirit, than that general discovery of God in Nature which is sometimes gratified with the name of Nature Mysticism. He is laying down a principle, at once metaphysical and psychological, by means of which we may hope to reduce to some kind of order the tangled witness of ' religious experience ' ; and sift out the facts which its phantasies veil and reveal. For now, having abandoned all demand for a clear-cut definition of the word ' Spirit ', and accepted instead its concrete and mysterious presence and our own fragmentary, uneven experience and response, we are brought to a further problem—How has man, a sense-conditioned creature committed to succession, come to be aware of this supersensual and unchanging Reality ? And we have already replied that this knowledge comes not by our own explorations but by the prevenient action and incitement of God-Spirit, by the entry of the Spaceless into space—in a broad sense, by revelation. Reality must stir and touch its half-made creature, before it can be desired. God must reach in to us, before we can reach out to Him. And St. John's doctrine gives us the path which we may expect that revelation to take.

In order to move the human soul with gentleness, Spirit makes Its approach, in a way at once majestic and humble, through the 'forms and images' of that sensible world to which we are adjusted and in which we are bathed. These forms, these creatures—just because they possess their own finite independence and reality, because they are true creations and not dreams—are capable of carrying the reality of the Infinite; providing, as it were, points of insertion for the self-giving energies of the all-enfolding supernatural world. Without some admixture of sense, like dust in sunny air, we are, says St. John again, almost incapable of perceiving the spiritual light. And were it not for this stooping down of the Infinite to the finite, this mingling of Spirit with sense, the direct impact of the Absolute might well shatter us. 'It is a dreadful thing to fall into the hands of the Living God.' Those veils and obscurities at which we sometimes cavil are the garments of mercy upon the Spirit of Holiness.

Looking with reverence on the human scene, and seeking to realize our situation, conditioned by the senses and yet susceptible to the deep currents of the spiritual world, we begin to perceive how wide is the field within which this principle of Spirit's

THE REVELATION OF SPIRIT 35

penetration of our spirits by way of the objects of sense can interpret our baffling glimpses and experiences of Reality. In the light of this principle, it is easy to recognize in the most deeply valued practices and hallowed objects of organized religion, points of insertion through which the quickening action of the Spirit can reach the faithful and receptive soul. And though this may not 'explain' the mysterious communications we call sacramental grace, at least we obtain a formula within which to place them. As a vast area of supernatural truth, still unexhausted by us, is condensed, focused, and flooded upon the natural world through the person of Christ —so, limited incarnations of Spirit take place through the symbolic and sacramental acts of religion. Récéjac's definition of mysticism as 'the tendency to approach the Absolute morally and by means of symbols' told only half the truth. It is also through and in symbols, bridging the chasm between sense and spirit, that the Absolute—without any reduction of an utter transcendence and otherness—makes Its merciful approach to the spirit of man. 'When that supernatural Light of which we speak', says St. John of the Cross, 'enters the soul in its simple purity, independent of all those intelligible things which are proportioned to our understanding, the understanding is not irradiated and sees nothing.' Hence the wise tenacity with which historical Christianity has clung to liturgic and sacramental embodiments of the Holy, and surrounded them with mystery and awe, is justified.

Hence too the inevitable impoverishment which follows their neglect or repudiation. How tiny, even at the best, these points of insertion must be, and how limited the communication in comparison with the Reality conveyed, will be apparent to all in whom arrogance has not reached the dimensions of disease. For they are adapted to the narrow capacity of the creature; and the communication received, though its substance be always whole and unchanging, will vary in its richness according to the heart to which it comes.

Christians must regard the historical Incarnation as the greatest of all such insertions of Spirit into history; and the transfigured lives of the Saints as guaranteeing its continuance in the world. Jesus Himself is ' incarnate by the Spirit ' : a metaphysical truth to which we sometimes fail to give full weight, for indeed there lies behind it the full pressure of the supernatural world. In His earthly life we see Spirit's action, in and through a human personality entirely God-possessed; the Absolute Life mingled with the sensible and contingent, and only in rare moments revealing Its presence and power. We see the rich and inexhaustible significance of actions and events which might never, without this relationship, have emerged from the flux of use and wont; but, seized upon as the stuff of revelation, now glow and deepen like an opal, which rewards our steadfast contemplation with new colour and new light. ' God the incomprehensible makes Himself comprehensible in this humanity,' says Bérulle, ' God the

THE REVELATION OF SPIRIT 37

ineffable becomes audible in the voice of His Word incarnate, and God the invisible is seen, in the flesh which He has united with the very nature of His Eternity.'

And thus, the lowly birth, the call and preaching of a local prophet, His communion with God and compassionate ministry among men, His conflicts with ecclesiastical authority, each detail of His betrayal and death—all this historical material, which is the substance of the plain narratives of the Synoptics, is lifted to a fresh order of significance. The events of Christ's life are well named ' mysteries ' for their meaning transcends the historical accidents and occasions which condition their outward form, and has an immortal relation with the interior life of men. There is a mounting revelation of the Spirit, in and through this uttered Thought, the incarnate Word. The point of insertion has behind it the wealth and pressure of the Infinite Life. So we should not accept the fragmentary narratives and simple insights of the New Testament writers as telling all the truth ; or reject as unhistorical the discoveries and interpretations of the saints. Centuries of meditation have widened and deepened the channel of revelation. The procession of the Spirit takes place in the Eternal order ; and through Bethlehem and Calvary, Hermon and the Upper Room, a wealth of life and light which is not yet exhausted comes to wide-open, self-oblivious souls. ' All these events ', says Bérulle, ' took place in certain circumstances ; but they endure, and are become present and perpetual, in another manner. They are past as regards their execution, but they are present as regards their power . . . the Spirit of God, whereby the Mystery was worked, is the abiding fact of which it is the outer vesture. His efficacy and power make the mystery operative in us, and He is ever living, actual, and present in it. This compels us to treat the things and mysteries of the Gospel, not as things past and dead, but as things living and present, and even eternal, from which we also must gather a present and eternal fruit.'

The principle here laid down—one aspect of that great law of the creative penetration of Spirit into sense on which all Christian philosophy is built—operates over the whole of the historical and institutional material of religion; indeed, over its literary and artistic material as well. All this, used with simplicity and meekness, can become the medium of spiritual communications which may far transcend the insights or intentions of those by whom it was first devised. The simplest facts of historical religion, or the commonplaces of devotional literature, subject to the penetrative action of Spirit, can thus acquire a transcendental reference; and enter the sacramental economy. Not merely the common experience of a constant new discovery of deep meaning in familiar acts and words, but that large range of phenomena which we are inclined to set aside because of their comparative rarity, fall under the general method by which, as St. John says, God

THE REVELATION OF SPIRIT

'sets a soul in movement' towards that centre which is Himself. Here we get a clue and can give a meaning to those 'openings' as the Quakers so excellently called them, well known to all who are accustomed to the meditative reading of Scripture and other spiritual books; when our 'condition' is directly met by way of words long familiar, but now suddenly lit up from within, transformed and enriched by the living Spirit which enters through this loophole our closely-shuttered minds. In such moments, a real communication of the Infinite to the finite takes place. 'There is in books', said the Divine voice to Thomas à Kempis, 'one voice and one letter that is read, but it informeth not all alike. For I am within secretly hidden in the letter, the Teacher of truth, the Searcher of man's heart.'

Few persons possessed of religious sensitiveness pass through life without experiencing such abrupt illuminations; which, transcending any psychological explanation, must be reckoned—however little we understand them—among the mysterious facts of the spiritual life. And it is, I think, by an extension of this same principle that we arrive at the interpretation of the more abnormal forms of religious experience. All those psychic automatisms which are loosely described as 'mystical phenomena'—voices, visions, the 'sense of Presence', the profound mono-ideism of the contemplative—are certainly susceptible of psychological explanation; and may witness to nothing more than the vigour of the subject's own fantasy-life.

But this does not invalidate them as possible points of insertion, through which Spirit acts on the soul. It is easy enough to adopt the lowest possible explanation of observed events ; but when these events are placed in their context, the inadequacy of this proceeding becomes plain. The significant fact is not that certain types of religious hallucination occur ; but that they can and sometimes do mediate the Transcendent. Thus any one who is inclined to mystical audition, even in the slight degree which precludes real hallucination, will recognize two facts. First, the immense authority that is felt to inhere in the message ; which is always abrupt and unexpected, and comes charged with a weight of significance out of all proportion to the simplicity of its form. Secondly, the close union between this entirely spiritual communication and the verbal formula in which it is received ; and which ever afterwards carries a certain sacramental reference. There seems to be a difference of degree, rather than of kind, between such an experience as this and the apparent reception of an other-worldly truth and light by Scripture 'openings'. When St. Francis, in absorbed contemplation of the Crucifix, heard the words 'Repair My Church', we may surely believe that here the guiding energy of Spirit touched and moved him, even though the form of the communication was supplied by his own sensory memories. But was this message more supernatural than that which he received when he sought to verify the vocation of Bernard of Quintavalle by the opening

THE REVELATION OF SPIRIT 41

of the Missal, and there found an equally clear command ? Both are impressive examples of the apparent action of Spirit in and through the channels of sense : a judgement that is supported by the series of events which they set in movement. They only differ by the fact that in the first case the sensory medium is provided by the experient's own mind ; while in the second it has objective existence.

And the same gradation can surely be observed in those apprehensions which use the machinery of sight. The glimmering Presence, deeply felt and almost seen, may be caught and held in the mesh of a pictured thought : whilst on the other hand, the sacred act or object which conveys ' otherness ' cannot be distinguished in principle from the image which is projected from the mind of the visionary to become a focus of transcendental feeling. Sometimes indeed the actual distinction between the contributions of Spirit and of sense becomes very thin ; and we realize how slight is its importance for us. Thus for St. Gregory or St. Thomas saying Mass, the material veil becomes transparent ; and within and beyond it they gaze entranced on the eternal Act, perceived under an image which is either visualized or apprehended without sight. And this double experience of the fusion of outward act and inward revelation is surely a typical instance of that general method, by which Spirit moves and teaches spirit : ' working man's perfection according to man's nature ' through the machinery of sense.

Here the soul trembles on the edge of something

it can never formulate. Sacred acts and phrases become charged with a supersensual light, in which at last they are lost. But it is because the act and the phrase have become condensers of the mysterious energy of Spirit, that the soul achieves by their help the subsequent transcendence of all apparent form. Nor need the poor quality of the condenser affect the experience it mediates. God-Spirit, Who is the indwelling principle of the outward mystery, acts through the form and image ; subduing to His purpose the adequate and the inadequate alike. The hymn which the highbrow rejects may yet become a channel of adoration ; and celestial love be recognized through the most deplorable efforts of religious art. The poorest picture, the crudest aspiration, then as it were becomes flood-lit from within ; charged with an unspeakable holiness. The sick man gazing hour after hour at and through a badly modelled Crucifix, and thus entering ever more deeply into the mystery of love and pain, has an experience of Spirit denied to the exquisite taste which rejects all images except the very best. The insistence of all contemplatives on a secret Divine teacher—as Bremond puts it, ' the fundamental and exclusively divine experience from which all else radiates '—helps us to a fuller understanding of all that is implied in this, and teaches us the justice of Bérulle's observation : ' Who would hold anything mean where all is so great, and where each thing, however small it may be, yet touches so closely Divinity Itself ? '

THE REVELATION OF SPIRIT

Nor does the origin, first meaning, or historic sanction of the conveying image matter very much. Those Psalms in which the soul finds mirrored its own intense experience, bore a wholly different meaning—sometimes more barbarous than religious—for those who used them first. Humble tunnelling will discover beneath the most unpromising landscape the spiritual gold. Many a dubious devotion has contributed to the formation of a saint. Our fastidious discriminations fade to insignificance before the overwhelming majesty of that generous Life and Love, which enters by these narrow portals the sense-conditioned life of men.

> O Lux beatissima,
> Reple cordis intima
> Tuorum fidelium.
>
> Sine tuo numine,
> Nihil est in homine,
> Nihil est innoxium.

What is the human creature, that it should make its little terms, either logical or aesthetic, in a bargain so wholly one-sided as this?

SPIRITUAL LIFE

I

CREATED SPIRIT

So now we turn from these scattered and tentative thoughts of God, the Absolute Spirit distinct and all-holy ; standing over against His human creatures, yet intimately present in every fibre of the soul. And we enter on a fuller consideration of our own case. ' My God and all ! What art thou and what am I ? ' said St. Francis. What is man, the derived, created spirit ? In what sense is that mysterious word to be applied to our strangely compounded human personality ?

It is a platitude that man is amphibious, a creature of the borderland ' set between the unseen and the seen '. He cannot be explained in physical terms alone, or spiritual terms alone ; but partakes of both worlds. But, like many other so-called platitudes, this one conveys a stupendous truth which is seldom fully realized by us : the truth of our unique status, our mysterious capacity for God. Man's relation to the animal world needs no demonstration. A stroll round the Zoo reveals plenty of disconcerting family likenesses. A very little introspection discovers animal instincts, politely disguised, in control of our normal behaviour. In moments of passion, the standards of the jungle still make an irresistible appeal. Physically we rank as a part of that rich and varied natural order, which is brought forth and maintained by the Divine Immanence. Yet on the other hand, we are called to witness to the Divine Transcendence. There is in us a ground and knowledge of Eternity, a thirst for ultimates, a penetrating sense of incompleteness which is the true cause of our secret unrest ; whatever the disguises it may assume. A certitude, a dim but real experience of another world and level of life, in contact with our deepest selves, grows with our interior growth. ' So foolish was I and ignorant, I was as a beast before Thee ; and yet, I am continually with Thee.' Beyond and within the web of temporal circumstance which seems to shut us in, is that steadfast brooding Presence, the Fact of all facts, Who is making us for Himself. Natural man may be subject to contingency, metaphysical man is in the Hand of God : and knowledge of this situation and all it must imply for us, deepens with our increase in spiritual sensitiveness. Anchored to this planet, with our obvious animal affinities and more obvious spiritual obscurities and limitations, we cannot describe ourselves or account for our mysterious situation, without recourse to other-worldly categories. When we penetrate beyond the sensible, we discover in ourselves a substantial life which is non-successive, non-extended ; we perceive ourselves to be derived

CREATED SPIRIT

spirits, somehow akin to the holy Spirit of all spirits, God. There is within us at least a crumb, a seed, which belongs already to the order of the timeless; yet cannot achieve its destiny, become fully real, without a gift from beyond itself. And here we find the basis in experience for all that religion means by prayer and grace—prayer, the Godward movement of the soul; and grace, the manward movement of God's Love.

' Man ', says Lionel Thornton, ' cannot evade the ultimate conviction that his true home is in the eternal order; and that his individuality was meant to reach its fulfilment through the transforming activity of that order on his life.' And the first meaning of a spiritual life is, that in it man accepts this marvellous intercourse as the ruling fact of his existence. He ceases to give exclusive attention to the passing, to pour himself out in response to the invitations of sense, and looks towards this, his true being; on one hand quietly receiving in his ground the action of God, on the other freely seeking to conform to the eternal order, instead of to the natural series alone. No psychology which ignores this double status and double response of the unstable psyche, poised between eternity and time, can give any intelligible explanation of human action and human desire.

Certainly our conscious hold on this spiritual heritage is still far less clear and certain than our hold on our physical heritage. Our powers have been developed in close contact with the senses, and by the pressure of the physical world, with its constant stimulation of the instinctive life. Clear correspondence with the other order must be the prerogative of a minority of souls, acting in the interests of the race. We may note certain facts, certain recurrent experiences, though we know little about them; and may seek to combine and present them under images. But we do this, not because we have any hope of reaching ultimate truth in these matters, but in order to tell souls how to act. All descriptions of the spiritual life are thus tentative and symbolic. They are road maps, not representations of reality. We move with comparative safety step by step; but we risk mountain sickness, if we raise our eyes too often to the awful landscape that surrounds us.

For our minds are so made that we can only realize Spirit vaguely and in patches; and only by the deliberate use of symbolic speech can give precision to our awareness. When we ascend in prayer to the soul's summit, we find we have come up to the frontiers of another life, in respect of which we are dependent, needy, dumb and dim of sight. Yet this abjection and this poverty are the very conditions of our happiness and wealth.

> Veni, pater pauperum.

So here Religion is justified in her insistence on the blessed state of the childlike and the humble: her constant reminder that what matters supremely is not our own exact degree of understanding, but the

CREATED SPIRIT 49

hold which the spiritual order has on us, and the power which flows from it through surrendered and self-oblivious personalities. In other words, in the great strange work of man's spiritualization the initiative ever lies with God and His Spirit, not with us. His priority is absolute. We realize, then, why the life of the spirit so often begins in a sense of personal incompleteness, of dependence and need: and why man's progress in spirituality, his interior growth, is felt at its deepest far more as a response to that Spirit's incitement than as a deliberate ascent to new levels of life. It is, in fact, an opening of the door of the finite to the Infinite Love, an increasing surrender to the subtle pressure of that Power ' which ever lifts and bears us ' ; not a self-actualized adventure of the independent will and heart, a pilgrim's steady progress from ' this world to that which is to come '.

' Unto Him who is everywhere ', says St. Augustine, ' we come by love and not by navigation.' Talk of the ' Mystic Way ' and its stages, or the ' degrees of love ', may easily deceive us unless the Divine immanence, priority, and freedom be ever kept in mind. We may think of the soul's essential being as ever lying within the thought of God ; and, equally, of His creative love as dwelling and acting within that soul's ground. These are contrasting glimpses of that total Truth ' of which no man may think '. And the true life of the spirit requires such a gradual self-abandonment to that prevenient and all-penetrating Presence that we become at last its unresisting agents ; are formed and shaped under its gradual pressure, and can receive from moment to moment the needed impulsions and lights.

Veni, lumen cordium.

Here we find a place for that mysterious attraction or compulsion which is perhaps the most striking of the ordinary evidences of the Holy Spirit's action on souls. The persistent inexplicable pressure towards one course—the curious attraction to one special kind of devotion or of service—the blocking of the obvious path, and the opening of another undesired path—all these witness to the compelling and moulding power of the living Spirit ; taking, and if we respond, receiving the gift of our liberty and our will.

This indeed is what the spiritual life has always seemed to the greatest, humblest, and most enlightened souls ; whatever symbols they may use in their efforts to communicate it. It is God, vividly and intimately present in all things and in us, ever setting the demand of His achieved Perfection over against the seething energies of His creative love, Who works in and through that world of things on us. And He demands our entire subjection to His creative action, our endurance of His secret chemistry ; that He may work through and in us on the world. We matter and our transformation matters, only in so far as we and it contribute to God's total purpose— the only thing that matters at all. This is the double truth which colours and harmonizes all the various

CREATED SPIRIT 51

strands of man's religious life, and finds intimate and detailed expression in the facts of conversion, vocation, and guidance. For by this secret action, so little understood, the fluid and changeable nature of man, at first conformed to that natural series within which our lives arise, is gradually subdued to the purposes of the Unchanging; to become at last a channel of Absolute Life, an agent of the Creative Will. The Psalter and the Christian liturgy, in which so much of that life is crystallized, and which possess the deep and genuine realism of all great works of art, are full of allusions to this absolute dependence; this confident hold on the Unseen, and its redeeming, cleansing action on the soul.

'O God make speed to save us. O Lord make haste to help us. . . . Prevent us O Lord in all our doings; further us with thy continual help. Raise up, we pray thee, thy power and come among us . . . that we may daily be renewed by thy Holy Spirit . . . that so we may be made partakers of the divine nature. . . . For with thee is the well of life and in thy light we see light. . . . Cleanse the thoughts of our hearts, by the inspiration of thy Holy Spirit. . . . Without thee we are not able to please thee. . . . Assist us with thy grace. . . . O what great troubles and adversities has thou shewed me! and yet didst thou turn and refresh me; yea, and broughtest me from the deep of the earth again.'

In these constantly repeated phrases, once their

profound realism is understood, we can hear the authentic voice of the human spirit. Like a recurring melody, they bind the Divine Office in one ; and make of it the supreme expression of the Godward confidence of men.

II

MAN NATURAL AND SUPERNATURAL

AS we get accustomed to our own psychology, grow in self-knowledge, we realize ever more deeply the fact—however we may express it—that our being has already its metaphysical aspect. There is a sense in which it is true to say that we are not all of a piece. The human creature seems to be poised uncertainly between two orders ; ' waiting the full adoption ', as St. Paul has it, into the spiritual sphere, yet already possessing the seed of that true being, which makes the spiritual sphere its destined home. Because partly adjusted to each order, it is not perfectly adjusted to either ; and this is the cause of its instability and its unrest. So the distinction which was first made by the Platonists, and runs through the spiritual literature of Christendom, between our ' higher ' and ' lower ' nature, our ' superior ' and ' inferior ' powers, does interpret and harmonize a wide range of human experience ; even though it may be incompatible with present fashions in psychology. In one form or another— and all its forms will be of course symbolic—we are obliged to adopt a two-story diagram of human nature in any attempt to describe the characters and incidents of the spiritual life. We must distinguish between the instinctive levels of the psyche, so obviously adjusted to our natural environment, so vigorous in their response to nature and their claims on all that nature has to give—and therefore so full of inconvenient factors, once the merely natural life is left behind—and the will and love which seek another country and acknowledge another claim. For these strangely assorted partners lust one against the other, and continue in their conflict; whatever new name their activities may receive. We may not agree as to the precise place where the boundary between them is established: but a boundary there has got to be.

If there is in us a depth and intensity of being, a 'spark of the soul' which inheres in God, there is none the less a ground of our life which is in close union with the animal realm and animal desire. In some, the tension between these two natures is acute; in others, one manifestly predominates. Even the most elementary attention to our own inner movements is enough to assure us of that; and supports the view of St. François de Sales, that failure to distinguish rightly between these two levels and their claims causes 'much confusion in the thoughts and actions of men'. The instinctive life of natural self-regard, obeyed without reflection or resistance, would at last lead downwards and outwards to the establishment of

MAN NATURAL AND SUPERNATURAL 55

a completely animal man; entirely given over to succession, acquisitive and combative in the interests of his own physical survival and well-being, lustful and ruthless in the interests of the survival of the race. The other life, the life of the 'higher powers' when they follow their true attraction, leads upwards and yet inwards towards the transcending alike of succession and of self-interest; to that new level of correspondence with Creative Spirit at which St. Paul hints in his mysterious sayings concerning the 'glorious liberty of the Children of God'.

And this unearthly orientation is possible to the creature, because of another, deeper and more awful truth. The constant references of spiritual writers to a certain vital centre of the soul—whether we call it 'root', 'ground' or 'apex'—where God, the Uncreated Spirit, dwells permanently and substantially, have genuine meaning, and point to a real fact; however symbolic or contradictory the language in which they are expressed. There is a deep heart in man, which the life of succession hardly stirs to consciousness, but which is maintained in a single undivided act of adherence to the Reality of God. Therefore in part at least we already belong to the unchanging world of Spirit; and no discussion of it can have value which does not begin with a humble recognition of the awful mystery hidden in our own hearts. 'In every soul, even that of the greatest sinner', says St. John of the Cross, 'God lives and substantially dwells. This sort of union between God and all creatures is an enduring fact.' But the Saint at once goes on to distinguish between this substantial immanence of the Creator in the creature, and that supernatural union which requires of the creature willed self-giving as the price of transformation, and is the essence of a spiritual life : impossible as this union would be, were it not for the prevenient act and presence of God.

'When we speak of the union of the soul with God, we set aside this substantial union common to all created beings, and have in view the transformation of the soul in God by love. . . . God is always really in the soul ; by His presence He gives and conserves its natural being ; but this does not mean that He always communicates to it supernatural being. This communication is the fruit of grace and love, and all souls do not enjoy it. Those who do, do not all possess it in the same degree, since their love may be greater or less. Hence we see that the greater the love, the more intimate is the union, which means that it is the conformity of our will to the Will of God which makes our union with Him more or less perfect. A will utterly conformed to Him, achieves perfect union and supernatural transformation in God.'

Everything we can say about the spiritual life is really a gloss and explication of this passage ; which answers with precision the question—'What *is* a spiritual life ? ' It is the life of a human creature which is being transformed in God by the joint action of His energetic grace and its own

MAN NATURAL AND SUPERNATURAL

faithful love : moving through many fluctuations to that condition in which, as Gerlac Petersen says, 'it worketh all its works in God, or rather God doth work His own works in it ; so that the soul worketh not so much itself, but rather is itself the work of God'. Hence this life as it grows brings ever wider ranges of our complex nature within the transforming sway of Holiness ; which enters the sanctuary of each human personality, there to evoke and nourish its Godward temper, and transform the crude substance of the ego as yeast transforms dough.

And perhaps we may say that for most men the first stage of that life begins at the point in which the all-penetrating immanent God makes Himself known to His creature ; and by the mysterious touch of His eternal Being wakes up that creature's transcendental sense. For in this same moment man becomes known to himself in a different way than ever before.

> All year long upon the stage
> I dance and tumble and do rage,
> So furiously I scarcely see
> The inner and eternal Me.

The inner and eternal Me—spirit, the metaphysical self, that most hidden and intimate ground of personality—this is the height or depth at which we desire God and taste God. With its awakening, the spiritual life begins. And once more, if we are to make sense of our experience, this germ of absolute being—which we humbly trust to be our truest selves—must in some way be distinguished from the 'I' of our surface activity and response. 'Souls, human souls', says Von Hügel, 'do not even begin to attain to their true unity, indeed they are not really awake, until they are divided up—until the spirit within them begins to discriminate itself against the petty self.' A genuine introspection will always achieve this discrimination. Below the natural and rational self of our surface experience, so nicely adapted to the world of succession, so ready to assume self-governing rights, we then become secretly aware of another, more fundamental life. The experience of the first self is of the contingent and successive; the experience of the second is of the immediate and the unchanging. This 'Me' is tuned to the mighty wave-lengths of the world of spirit; as 'I' is tuned to the quickly-changing world of sense. And even though we are bound to agree with St. John of the Cross that 'being spirit, the soul has neither upper nor lower part, nor can there be in her one region deeper than another, as in bodies which are extended in space, for her interior does not differ from her surface, since her nature is uniform throughout'—nevertheless, we are driven to spatial images and distinctions, always deceptive and often inconsistent though they be, in order to describe her experiences and discriminate that 'ground' or 'fine point' of the spirit, the real seat of the religious instinct, at which man knows his own true being and tastes God.

MAN NATURAL AND SUPERNATURAL

Deep in every soul there is a little chamber, where great stillness reigns and the torrent of succession seems to cease. And though the term of our spiritual growth must surely be the unification of the whole nature ' in the bonds of love ',—the opening of the door of the inner fastness so that the music of its quiet reaches every corner of the home—it does begin in the clear recognition of this cleavage, this difference in kind between the life of spirit tuned to eternity and the life of sense tuned to time. For the life of sense is always at the mercy of inward passion and external accidents. It is for ever falling down into multiplicity ; is claimful, turbulent, uneven. But in the ' upper region of the soul ', says Caussade, ' God and His Will produce an Eternity always even, always uniform, always still. In this wholly spiritual region, where the uncreate, the indistinct, the ineffable keep the soul at an infinite distance from all the shadowy multiplicities of the created world, we abide in peace even though the senses be given over to the storm '.

First from one angle and then from another, all the great teachers of the spiritual life seek a formula which can express their deep conviction of this twofold nature of man—these partners which should complete each other, but are more often at war. They feel that those levels of consciousness which are in close alliance with the physical, and so more or less at the mercy of sense-impressions and instinctive movements, and give us material which can be dealt with by logical thought, must be distinguished from those which seek—virtually or actually—the Vision of the Principle, beyond logical thought. ' Sensitive nature ' is turned earthwards and selfwards. The ' fine point ' of the spirit is turned Godwards. And two sorts of knowledge are felt to belong to these two levels of life. One is clear, detailed, practical : it deals with the world which the senses show us. The other is luminous, universalized, indistinct : but it assures us of the unchanging realities of Spirit, baffling and attracting the soul. At its highest it is, as the mystics say, a ' tasting wisdom ', the indivisible fulfilment of contemplation and of love. And in certain mysterious activities and interests of man—in poetry, art, music, above all in the sacramental acts of visible religion—the two forms of knowledge mingle ; and news from the world of Spirit is conveyed by the channels of sense. How best to define the contrast and unity which exists between these two levels of life, and between the two forms of knowledge which we attribute to ' intuition ' and to ' thought ', is a permanent problem of religious psychology.

The human sense of God, the craving for eternal life, the metaphysical passion of the soul stretching from fear through wonder to delight—this, whatever aspect we choose to emphasize, whatever name we use, is the distinctive character of man. Here we discover the embryonic characters which point to his spiritual destiny. This stretching-out of the self towards something which lies beyond

MAN NATURAL AND SUPERNATURAL 61

succession and beyond sense—this 'metaphysic of the saints'—is the fact which lies at the root of all religion. 'To Thee do I lift up mine eyes O Thou that dwellest in the heavens!' Even if that only happened once, it would make a determinist view of reality very difficult. But as a matter of fact it happens again and again: and the real work in us of that balanced discipline of prayer and self-conquest which is the essence of a spiritual life, is to close the gap—sometimes wide, sometimes narrow, always deep—between sensitive nature, swayed by instinct and full of conflict and disquiet, and the soul's ground or apex, which is turned towards God and desires God.

A fully expanded spiritual life need not be one which seems to the world given over to the obvious practice either of devotion or good works. But it must be given over with a generous docility to the total purposes of Spirit; correctly adjusted to reality. Bit by bit the all-demanding Spirit must achieve undivided sway over the surface-I, as well as over the eternal Me: harmonize and weld them into a single instrument of the Will. The life of the Me is an essential prayer. Its very existence consists in an adherence to God. The ceaseless unexpressed aspiration of its being is that *Fiat mihi secundum verbum tuum* which opens the gate of the heart to the Absolute Life. And this essential prayer is to overflow into those restless and insurgent 'lower powers' which correspond with the world of the senses; calming, steadying, strengthening and enlightening, and creating a complete personality which shall be a free yet dependent centre of the Divine creative life. For the goal of our spiritual growth is not some special beatitude, some peculiar condition of awareness, but humble and useful co-operation with God. When we understand this, the stages and incidents of that growth are better understood, its sufferings and derelictions fall into place. All are seen to result from the dependence of our little spirits on God's infinite Spirit, and to be ways in which that Spirit works in and through us, to the accomplishment of a hidden design. For Man, says St. Thomas, 'in so far as he is moved to act by the Spirit of God, becomes in a certain sense an instrument of God'; and every phase of the spiritual life can be brought under this law. And it is a chief paradox of that life that its growth in power and initiative, its capacity for heroic and creative action, advances step by step with the creature's realization of a total responsibility and yet a total dependence upon God—energizing deeply and freely, but in perfect self-abandonment to the one Divine energy and act. 'I live, yet not I.'

III

CREATIVE SPIRIT

WE cannot, as Von Hügel said, find God's Spirit 'simply separate' from our own spirit; since the one impossibility of thought is the leaving of the thinking self behind. Still less can we isolate and observe that spirit, that seed of Absolute Life which is in us, apart from the supporting, spaceless, penetrating God. To speak of our spiritual life and our spiritual growth, then, is to speak not of ourselves but of Him; for we are daring to behold and describe the Divine creative action in its most subtle and mysterious operation, working in 'intimate union with our own'. It is true that there are many ways and degrees in which we may discover this fact of the ceaseless action of Spirit upon spirit; mediated as it is through all those physical and psychological experiences which make up the texture of our lives. One way or another, in times of crisis, in sudden moments of clear vision, in the terrible embrace of ghostly suffering—or by gradual meditation on the sequence of events, the slow insistent pressure, which changes the contour of our life, giving it a shape and meaning of which we never dreamed—

we become aware of the presence of an Infinite Fact, living, personal, inerrant ; whose moulding influence reaches us through and in that finite environment to which our outer lives are tuned.

We know the mysterious power of influence between man and man ; know it so well, that we seldom pause to think of its strangeness and significance—how decisively it witnesses against any theory of the soul as an independent monad. Yet this interpenetration of human spirits is a mere shadow of the deep and actual penetration and influence of God on souls. And though news of this steadfast creative action, this supporting and stimulating presence of God must—like all our other news—enter the field of consciousness through the senses or the intellect, translating intuition into concepts and sensible signs ; these only partly reveal and certify that deep action of Spirit upon and within our spirits, which is literally the life of our life. Sometimes it seems that we are bathed in a living Ocean, that pours into every corner of our being to cleanse, heal and refresh. Sometimes it seems that a personal energy compels, withstands, enlightens or suddenly changes us ; working on our stubborn natures with a stern, unflinching love. Yet even this language, vague as it may seem, is still far too rigid and too spatial, and these contrasting images too harsh and incomplete, for a situation and experience which only the allusive methods of poetry or inspiration can suggest.

There is on the north porch of the Cathedral of

CREATIVE SPIRIT 65

Chartres a wonderful sculpture of the creation of Adam. There we see the embryonic human creature, weak, vague, half-awakened, not quite formed, like clay on which the artist is still working : and brooding over him, with His hand on His creature's head, the strong and tender figure of the Artist-Creator. Creative Love, tranquil, cherishing, reverent of His material, in His quiet and patient method : so much more than human, yet meeting His half-made human creature on its own ground, firmly and gradually moulding it to His unseen pattern, endowing it with something of His own life. It is a vision of the Old Testament seen in the transfiguring light of the New Testament. The *I will* of an Absolute Power translated into the *I desire* of an Absolute Love ; awful holiness reaching out to earthly weakness, and wakening it to new possibilities. Now this situation is surely the situation of all living souls ; and the very essence of their spiritual life is or should be the lifting up of the eyes of Adam, the not yet fully human creature who is being made, in his weakness and hope, to the holy creative love which never lets him go, and in which his life is to find its meaning and goal.

It is true that the half-awakened Adam, stirring to consciousness, can give no exact meaning to the strange experiences that seem to reach him : the sudden or gradual changes, sharp pinches, smooth pressures or enlargements, by means of which he is being conformed to the secret type. He is still rather dazed by his situation ; Eden itself is not clear to him yet. The true character of the Divine action is blurred by its passage through the world of succession. He sees and feels the Potter's tools, but not the Potter's hand 'acting within the world and moving all things to their respective ends'. Yet in prayer he can at least look up towards the Power that holds him, and so glimpse the truth of that majestic and delicate action; working through circumstance, 'from one end to another, mightily and sweetly ordering all things', and bringing each created spirit to its appointed state. This humble glance from the successive to the Abiding—this is the first gesture of recognition, the first spiritual movement of man.

Thinking of this we begin to realize what is meant by Maritain's deep saying : 'Adam sinned when he fell from Contemplation—since then, there has been a cleavage in man's life'. For sin is the willed departure of man's spirit from correspondence with the Spirit of God ; a thwarting of the creative ideal. And such a thwarting of life's purpose is to be expected, when man ceases to look up and out beyond the world : to lift his eyes to God. Then he makes a cleavage between vision and action, departs from that realistic sense of the overruling Divine action, that 'Vision of the Principle' as St. Gregory called it, which is the first point of a spiritual life. Though the Vision of the Principle is far too great for Adam, and produces, by its very radiance, the obscurities of faith—still this dim humbling disclosure of the mystery of God's action

CREATIVE SPIRIT

does make the creature more supple to the pressure of the Divine life.

Yet even so, perhaps the image is not quite complete ; nor the situation rightly seen by us. For spiritual life consists in a submission, which is by turns active and passive, to the moulding and penetrating action of the supernatural order. It requires a secret collaboration between the soul and God. The gradual growth and transformation of the half-made natural creature into an agent of the Divine creativity—a ' child of God '—is achieved by a ceaseless and ever purer correspondence of man's will with the Creative Power. Left to ourselves, we are wholly unable to rise above our normal correspondence with the world of succession ; the sensitive and natural levels of life. Spiritual life begins with a recognition of this humbling truth, and a willing response to that Spirit already intimately present with us, Who ' first creates and then sustains and stimulates ' our childish souls, balancing each gift by a demand. It is, above all, the touch of this Creative Spirit acting on and through us, that we mean when we speak of our ' experience of God '.

What this experience can be in depth and richness for a fully expanded religious sense, is realized when we read with humility the declarations of the saints ; for instance, when St. Teresa tells us that it marked an epoch in her spiritual life when she ' learned that God was present in and with her Himself ; and not, as she had been told, by His grace '. For here is a concrete experience, reported with a realistic simplicity, of the sustaining and stimulating action of that Present God. Those words are not chosen haphazard; they represent two distinct groups of experiences, in which we recognize the penetration of Spirit into sense, the direct action of God on human personality. First that steady support which, as Plotinus says, 'ever bears us', whether we notice it or not : as true an operation of the Holy Spirit as any abnormal manifestation, or 'charismatic' gifts. Next that strange insistent pressure, reaching men sometimes through outward events, sometimes by interior ways, which urges them forward on the spiritual path, incites them to those particular efforts, struggles and sacrifices, through which they grow up in the supernatural life. For this life requires from us a response which seems a paradox : on one hand an utter self-abandonment to the sustaining power ; and on the other hand, because of that abandonment, a vigorous personal initiative—a ceaseless balance and tension, through and by which our human action, ever more fully laid open to the Spirit, at last becomes part of the deep action of God.

This twofold relation of God's infinite Spirit and man's finite spirit is reflected in our characteristic religious practices : works of art, born of the deep Christian instinct for reality, which always seem to carry a double reference. On one hand there is the constant acknowledgement of a solid and objective support given by the Immanent Holy to

CREATIVE SPIRIT

its feeble creature—a literal response to the great Advent prayer ' Raise up, we pray thee, thy power ; and come among us '. On the other hand, there is the steady demand on the self's own initiative and courage ; on costly willing action, a total self-donation in the interests of Spirit, which may fulfil itself by way of homely self-denials or faithful unconsoled devotion, or may reach the summits of heroic sacrifice. Man, the slave of the Highest, is to be at once the patient and the agent of the Unseen. As that communion in which he receives the Food of eternal life is given the characters of a sacrifice ; so every true procession of the Spirit unites a gift and a demand. The Power comes first to transform, and then to use, the creature ; to call out and penetrate its natural energies, and dedicate them to supernatural ends. For the dignity of the human soul is this : that not only can it be transformed in God by, as we say, co-operation with His grace, but being transformed, living eternal life, it can also take its part as the agent and tool of God in the redemptive action of the Holy on the world. And in this correspondence, so richly creative, with that Spirit which gives all that it is, and takes all that we are, we find once more the secret rhythm and deepest meaning of the spiritual life.

IV

LIFE FINITE AND INFINITE

AS we watch life, we realize how deeply this double fact of God's inciting movement and the response it evokes from us, enters into all great action ; and not only that which we recognize as religious. In all heroic achievements, and all accomplishment that passes beyond the useful to seek the perfect, we are conscious of two factors which cannot be separated but cannot be confused. There is ever a genuine and costly personal effort up to the very limit of the self's endurance : and there is, inciting, supporting and using this devoted thrust of the creature, this energetic love, a mighty invading and enveloping Power. So too in all great historic and religious movements, we seem to discern a secret incitement of the corporate action, a hidden Providence, subduing to its purpose the varied energies of men.

For this double strain—this re-inforcement of the temporal by the eternal, and this using of the temporal as a medium for the Absolute Action of God—is present in all history ; though perhaps specially clear in the religious history of man. It is vividly present in the birth of the Christian Church at

LIFE FINITE AND INFINITE

Pentecost, and in the subsequent events of the period so rightly called charismatic. There we see on one hand the utter dependence of the small creature-spirits on the Infinite Life, with its pressure and its prohibitions. On the other hand, we see the self-oblivious courage and initiative, the unlimited confidence and hope of those same limited creatures, called to incarnate something of that Infinite Spirit's will. ' Greater is he that is in you than he that is in the world ' says the Johannine writer, referring to a recognized truth of experience.

Were we more sensitive to the delicate forces that enmesh and penetrate us, we should feel the operation of that Spirit within all circumstance ; increasing in power and clearness with the degree of surrender achieved by those who are its instruments. For the Spirit does not work on our small spirits by way of suppression, but by way of enhancement ; and the more complete its conquests, the more plainly does this truth appear. The saints are not examples of a limp surrender. In them we see dynamic personality using all its capacities ; and acting with a freedom, originality and success which result from an utter humility, complete self-loss in the Divine life. In them supremely, will and grace rise and fall together ; the action of the Spirit stimulates as well as sustains, requiring of them vigorous and often heroic action, and carrying them through desperate sufferings and apparently impossible tasks. No man was ever more fully and consciously mastered by the Spirit than St.

Paul; and we know what St. Paul's life was like. The same is true of St. Hildegard, St. Francis, St. Catherine of Siena, St. Vincent de Paul. 'The human will', says Dr. Temple, 'is a more adequate instrument of the Divine will than any natural force'. Even more truly we might say that the human spirit, transformed by love, is the most adequate instrument known to us of the Holy Spirit of God—the active energy of the Divine Love operating in time.

'I only want one thing,' said Elizabeth Leseur, 'the accomplishment of your will, in me and by me'. Since the essence of man is his will and his love, that quiet saying—so easily dismissed as a bit of piety—sums up the human soul's peculiar destiny, and the very aim of a spiritual life. Meek self-abandonment to the vast and hidden purposes of the Spirit, and vigorous selfless action as the result, are the poles between which the living soul is called to move. And because it is inherent in our limited freedom, that our acceptance of this destiny is, in the last resort, left to us—for the Divine incitement stirs but never overrules Its creature's will—the soul's responsibility over against God is absolute.

In the fourteenth Canto of the *Paradiso*, Dante gives a wonderful picture of the heavenly state of all courageous souls. It is not a state of mere security or passive bliss. He sees the joyful spirits of brave saints—those who took risks, faced suffering, solitude and darkness, the chivalry of the Spirit of

LIFE FINITE AND INFINITE 73

God—dwelling within a great Cross of Light. They flash to and fro on their various occasions; some upwards to God Pure, and some outwards to His creation. Each is self-given to his peculiar mission; but within the boundaries of one sacrificial Love, which unites them with its action, and fills them with its life. Entrance into that order, union with that life-giving life: this is the goal of our spiritual growth. For where this surrender is absolute, the mighty creative action evokes, develops and uses to the last drop Its creature's energy; and the result is such an amazing transcendency, such creative and redeeming power, as we see in the saints, whose spirit 'clothes and expresses' the Holy Spirit of God.

Thus a constant balance of surrender and initiative, a God-impelled action and a God-desiring contemplation, in ever-varying degrees and forms; this is the mark of a spiritual maturity. And because this ceaseless tension so easily overstrains us, and so easily opens the door to self-willed interpretation of the Creative Will, some corporate action and submission to the common judgement is needed too. The separate member must be knit up into that Mystical Body which is the organ of the great Divine action in the world. It is within this supernatural economy that all our little activities, religious and other, go forward; it is this informing aim which gives them worth; and it is this solemn consciousness of supporting and inciting Spirit,— at once *Patria* and *Pater*, but in its fullness ever remaining inexpressible—which is the mark of the really religious man.

We see then that the working of the Spirit on human personality, and the spiritual life which develops as a result of this commerce between finite and Infinite will, can never be identified with the abnormal phenomena or cataclysmic conversions too often described as ' religious experience '. We have indeed no reason to suppose that the supernatural world is less steady, less dependable in its operations than the natural world. Anything abrupt or sensational in our realization of Spirit is rather to be attributed to our weakness and instability, our sense-conditioned psychic life, than to the deep and quiet working of the Power of God. In the Book of Acts we have one of the greatest of all historic records of the Spirit's double action : felt sometimes as an invading, dictating, and transfiguring power, in sharp contrast with the ordinary levels of experience, but more deeply recognized in the continuous action and growth of individuals and groups indwelt by Him. And so with us. There may be italicized periods of either joy or abasement, when the reality and claim of God are suddenly and violently felt, and the Spirit seizes the field of consciousness ; and throughout the whole spiritual course, for some temperaments, moments of communion when His presence is vividly experienced, and His direct guidance is somehow recognized. But what matters far more is the continuous normal action, the steady sober growth which the Spirit

LIFE FINITE AND INFINITE

evokes, and cherishes if we are faithful : the whole life of correspondence between man the creature and the Absolute Will.

Thus the 'coming of the Holy Spirit', whether understood as a historic or a personal experience, does not mean any change in the Presence and Action of God ; but does mean a change in the attitude and capacity of men.

> O Lux beatissima,
> Reple cordis intima
> Tuorum fidelium.

'Your opening and His entering', said Meister Eckhart, 'are one moment.' The New Testament shows us men's experience of Christ as opening a door for the further experience of the energizing Spirit of God, 'as He is everywhere and at all times ' ; and ordinary human beings moving out to the very frontiers of human experience, to become channels of that Spirit's action in space and time. Since we are part of the society to which this happened and can happen still, our own responsibility as agents of Spirit is both individual and corporate ; and each reacts on the other. Church and soul are both temples of the living Reality of God. Prayer is the responsive moving-out of soul and of Church, to the Spirit whose first movement has initiated this marvellous intercourse between the finite and Infinite life.

Hence the true aim of the creature's transformation, is to weld that creature into the universal creative process—to make of each soul a new centre of creative life. Thus from the first all self-regarding spirituality, all mean ideals of safety and of comfort, are to be abandoned. The goal is not moral goodness, effective service, spiritual knowledge; but a whole life of adoring love, transcending and including all these ends. 'Salvation' means this total glad self-offering, this dedication of the whole drive of our nature and its incorporation into the eternal order; not for our own sake, but for the sake of the whole. And clearly nothing short of the immense attraction of that order, the steady pull and pressure of the Love of God, could persuade men to the sufferings and dedications involved in such a destiny as this. For the flame of Living Love is not a mild and tempered radiance. It burns as we approach, and only gives us of its ardour and its glory when we dare to plunge into its very heart. Perhaps all earth's lesser demands and vocations, the sacrificial call of truth and beauty, the passion of the explorer or the mountaineer, overriding selfishness and ease, are parts of the intricate process by which souls are trained for the supreme self-giving of eternal life.

So we arrive at this point. If the substantial reality of the human soul abides in that quality or *ens* we call spirit; and if here, in its ground or at its spire-point, it finds God dwelling, and its own real abiding place in Him—two sides of one truth—then growth in the spiritual life and entrance into reality, are the same thing. The disciplines of the

LIFE FINITE AND INFINITE

interior way become of immense importance for the unfinished creature we call 'man'. Every human being, said Péguy, represents a 'hope of God'. In less poetic terms, every human being is a potential spiritual personality, who can by faithful correspondence with God become an actual spiritual personality. The Church is a society of souls at every stage of growth, and adapted to a myriad different ends, yet all surrendered to the one indwelling Presence, and in all of whom this transformation is going forward 'as He wills'. Thus they form together in a special sense, a tabernacle, an organic embodiment for the Holy Eternal Spirit in space and time; one Body of many members—*Corpus Christi*.

V

THE GIFTS OF THE SPIRIT

'LOVE', says St. John of the Cross, ' is an inclination of the soul : an outgoing force or faculty, which makes it capable of ascending towards God.' Its true nature is not touched by any description which stresses its emotional quality. It is the whole thrust and drive of a conscious selfhood towards a desired object and end. Love then, says St. John again, ' is the medium which unites the soul to God. Thus love is the substance of a spiritual life. The higher the soul mounts in the degrees of love, the more profoundly she enters into God and identifies herself with Him. So, each stage in the soul's growth in love represents a fresh centre, each more interior than the last, wherein she can dwell in God. It is thus we can interpret the words " In my Father's house are many mansions " in their relation to the life of prayer '.

Hence, the soul which is fully given to the spiritual life, whatever her stage of growth and liability to fluctuation, has contracted as it were a ' habitude of love '. God has become for her the business of businesses ; the focus of interest. She possesses

THE GIFTS OF THE SPIRIT

at least in germ a permanent disposition or inclination, away from self-interest and towards self-abandonment to Him; an inclination which is comparable to the moral man's inclination to right conduct, or the artist's inclination to creativity. No one of these types is fully harmonized or fully alive, save when conformed to the demands of the ruling *habitus*. Nor does the Christian know that active peace which is the cause of happiness, until he is surrendered to that habitude of love, which constitutes in its perfection the supernatural charity of saints. For this habitude of love, the secret spring of all real prayer, is the same thing as that 'recollection' of which contemplatives speak as the temper of their whole existence and implied basis of their art.

'If', says Osuna, 'we accustomed ourselves to turn with intense love directly to the Divinity, attending to nothing else, and regulating our likings wisely, our love would penetrate all else until it reached Him, turning neither to the right nor to the left . . . this is true recollection, for the powers of the soul collect together and help one another, so that they may devote themselves unwearyingly to the work.' Such recollected love places the soul at the disposal of the 'rapting Spirit', directs its whole will along one channel; subordinates its being, wide-open and desirous, to the transforming penetration of the supernatural life, the golden shower. All the apparatus of devotion, in so far as it concerns the nurture of the individual spirit, tends to increase in it this habitude of humble self-abandoned love—'the affectionate and orderly direction of the will to the supreme Good', says Osuna again, 'so that the whole heart and feelings rush towards Him more swiftly than a stone descends to the centre of the earth'. And growth in the spiritual life is perhaps best measured by the degree in which it opens up human personality to this all-penetrating divine action, places the created spirit more and more at the disposal of the Immanent Spirit; so that the self's separate activity is more and more absorbed, transfused and possessed by God. And this is surely what we must expect, if the Christian doctrine of the Holy Spirit—the indwelling of the creature by the Godhead, under Its attribute of purposive love—be true.

The mind and soul of a mature man of prayer has simplified its gaze, and deepened and broadened its correspondences with Reality; and the result is seen in a peculiar confidence in the universe, a profound and peaceful acceptance of experience in its wholeness, and not only in purely religious regard. Such a soul—though it may and commonly does remain inarticulate as regards its deepest findings—is aware of the mysterious movements and pressures of the Spirit, and knows existence in a way others do not. Because of its humble and disciplined communion with that immanent Spirit, it has achieved a flexibility which can move to and fro between the inward and the outward; finding in both in the most actual sense, and ever more

THE GIFTS OF THE SPIRIT 81

and more in proportion to its self-abandonment, the presence of a living, acting God. It is this loving discernment of Reality through and in prayer, this ever-expanding experience of God, which is meant by the phrase ' mystical theology ' as employed by the great Christian masters of the spiritual life. For the treasure of God is not what we call ' simple ' ; given, and possessed by the soul, in a single act. There is a new gift, and a new revelation of reality each time the soul reaches a new centre of love. Yet each new centre seems to that loving soul to possess an ultimate quality : to be the fruition of all it is able to desire and receive.

And the transforming Divine influence, quickening and moulding the surrendered spirit, gradually produces within it certain characters which already belong to the transcendent order, and shall enable it for the living of the spiritual life. When theology speaks, in its special language, of the ' gifts ' of the Spirit, as the essential marks of the spiritual man, the reference seems to be to the emergence of these peculiar qualities in those in whom there is established the habitude of other-worldly love. They are qualities so alien to the normal temper of the sense-conditioned creature, that they seem indeed to be gifts infused from another level of reality ; involving correspondence with another kind of life.

> Da tuis fidelibus,
> In te confidentibus,
> Sacrum septenarium

With the soul's growth in docility and in courage, the enlargement of its interior life, the increase of its sensitiveness, its faithful submission to the cleansing power of events, it becomes ever more capable of receiving from the supernatural order these characters; enduing with the quality and colour of eternity the daily life of men. Every time a fresh centre is reached in that gradual journey to the depths of loving self-abasement, which is the only safe pathway to the heights of the Divine, a fresh emission of these transforming characters into the soul takes place and must take place: enhancing its delighted adoration, its devotedness, its strength, its supernatural lights. For growth in the spiritual life consists solely in an increase of God and decrease of self; becoming at its term a pure capacity for Him. Therefore the inflow of the 'gifts', the qualities of the supernatural life, keeps pace with the soul's increase in love. For God in His substantial Being indwells from the first her very substance, and the pressure of His Thought and Love will penetrate and transform her, in proportion to the active and loving abandonment, the self-forgetful willingness to suffer, which opens up her most secret recesses to His fire and light: the humble and desirous courage with which she says 'Come!'

We observe that these gifts—those ingredients of the spiritual creature, which shall make it like to God—are, as disclosed by their action on the psyche, quiet and steady things. They work in it a deepening and enrichment which are marked, not by any violent and emotional reactions, not by abnormal experiences, but by an increase in awe and devotedness ; in knowledge, wisdom, insight, strength. They do not come to destroy human nature, but to fulfil it ; lifting it to fresh levels of reality and power. And this is achieved not by the abrupt insertion of the unnatural ; but by the touch of a transforming grace on the natural. So humbly is the hand of God subdued to the material in which He works.

Fear of the Lord, Awe, that initial step in religious realism which puts the imperfect spirit into right relation with the Transcendent Perfect—this, the first gift of the Spirit, is in truth the sublimation and direction to God of man's creaturely sense. To know our own place over against the Holy, the utter contrast between the beauty of the Perfect and our natural state, our dependence and our nothingness before God, is the beginning of that Wisdom which shall be perfected on the heights of the contemplative life. For the first daunting revelation of Spirit, as wholly other than anything the creature can conceive or understand, kills at their root all the amiable sentimentalisms and shallow rationalisms of this-world religion ; and prepares the ground in which the supernatural virtue of humility, the very stuff of holiness, can grow. '. . . The Presence of God', says Huvelin, 'is proved by the confusion of the creature ; and by the desire that she has, tiny though she be, to do something for Him who has done all.' Thus the soul's most perfect prayer, over against that Absolute, is always *Nescevi! nescevi!* It is not the sinner but the saint, whose eyes have been opened on the world of spirit, who really knows himself ' carnal, sold under sin '. He has received the primal gift of Fear ; and in the light of the Eternal sees things as they are, and the nothingness of all man's theological constructions and spiritual experiences over against the splendour of God. Here the deepest abasement and most delighted adoration are one.

And this habitude of awe, this creaturely sense, is balanced and completed by the beautiful temper of Piety ; the darling grace of the religious soul, the expression of its perfect filial relationship, the transformation of our tender emotion in God. ' *Porro pietas cultus Dei est, nec colitus ille nisi amando* ', says St. Augustine. If awe be the soul's natural gesture over against the unmeasured majesty of Spirit, the solemn stillness of Eternity, Piety represents its childlike affection ; its delighted recognition of the fatherhood of the God whom it adores. Ruysbroeck, in his account of the ' gifts ' which transform the Godward-tending spirit, says that Piety gives to us a steadfast gentleness of heart. It means the docile acceptance and loyal application of the family point of view. So does the human spirit achieve a small share in the immense charity of God, poured out upon just and unjust, and an affectionate subordination to His purposes ; thus becoming more full of the Divine life-giving life, and more like God, as it broadens and deepens in

THE GIFTS OF THE SPIRIT 85

self-spending love. So the habitude of awe and the habitude of *pietas* expand the growing spirit in two directions; up to God Pure in humblest worship, and out in loving compassion towards His self-revelation in men. If total abasement before the Transcendent Perfect be ever one essential of man's spiritual life, an actual adoption into the order of supernatural charity is its completion. And both must go on increasing; ever more fully given within the growing soul. Piety is the spirit in which the Christian gives the cup of cold water, and so endues altruism with worship and turns it towards God. These tempers of the soul complete each other, like the vertical and horizontal arms of the Cross: and since in both spirit tends toward Spirit, they are infinite in their reach.

Because the awe and filial action of the creature must constantly come into play, and that within the concrete and confusing circumstances of life, a certain road-sense, a knowledge which is of the Spirit and casts the light of eternity on the problems of the temporal order, becomes essential to our spiritual health. For we have somehow to discern the true way of the Lord from among the tangled lanes and the arterial highways which run in every direction or none: must learn to distinguish the enduring reality from the spiritual sham. This deep experimental knowledge of the things of God—at the opposite pole from all notional spirituality, all religious cleverness—develops and becomes more precise as we seek to apply it. Thus the third change worked by creative Spirit in the creature given to prayer, is a gradual clarification of the judgement, an opening of the eyes upon Eternity—so that man begins to see the things that really belong to his blessedness, and separate the solid food of the spirit from the mere confectionery of faith.

Yet this enlightening alone—this knowledge of what to do and what to leave undone—is not enough for us. When the soul gets to grips with its vocation, it finds that self-transcendence is a hard and a heroic job. It is true that much work is done on and in it ; but always by way of a co-operation with its own effort, which demands the exercise up to the limit of its courage, endurance and love. Always, too, in the open under conditions of varying weather—dark wintry days, dry seasons, gales and fog. And the calm and selfless steadiness ' deflected neither by gladness nor by grief ', which must now be produced in us; accepting in tranquillity those alternations of joy and grief, hope and fear, profit and loss, good weather and bad, by which the soul is tempered—this belongs to God and is the answering gift to a maturing love. The mere habit of fortitude, the virtue of the hiker, slogging on after the first freshness is spent—even this essential disposition will hardly be established without the stimulus and the support of grace : still less, that ghostly strength which must carry the spirit safely over the most lonely and terrible stretches of the way. For here the small, bewildered and half-conscious soul—a little scrap of creation, inexplicable to itself—realizes its position among the dim and terrible mysteries of a universe that goes marching on, hard, cold, inexorable, unexplained. The valley of the shadow of spiritual death closes in on it, the conscious experience of faith is withdrawn. Man the spiritual creature is hemmed in by the natural; and cannot for the time escape its iron conditions. In his tiny way, he shares the blackest experience of the Cross. That pain and darkness, the whole mystery of the world's helplessness and sin, stands ever over against Holiness; its dread pressure is felt more and more, with the spirit's growth in purity and love. Thus the strength of the Transcendent must invade Its creature, if that creature is to bear the stresses of its great task, and operate as a tool of the Perfect in the warfare against evil in the world.

So even from its inception, man's spiritual life will be coloured by an awe-struck reverence and a filial love, as turn by turn he gazes out in contemplation of the Holy Reality, and returns to a humble but actual co-operation with that Spirit who is Father and Keeper of his soul. And with the growth of this habitude of adoration and of tender loyalty, there grows also a deepening insight, and an otherworldly strength. The human mind is purged, the human will is braced, by the tonic energies of love.

These are the 'ordinary' gifts of Spirit to spirit. Beyond them lie those three great characters which form the triple crown of an established holiness.

That sure intuition of the saints, who have learned the art of listening to the whisper of the Spirit in Whom they live, and in Whom all things are one: who are counselled by God in every circumstance, never at a loss, because entirely docile to the inner guidance. That ghostly understanding, undeceived by appearance, which pierces to the reality of every situation, shares ever more fully the Divine point of view, God's wide and loving understanding of all life. Last, the gift of Wisdom, that 'touch or stirring of God' says Ruysbroeck, which is the very substance of contemplation; tasting Him, savouring as it were the very flavour of Reality, and gradually spreading its mysterious influence over all the activities of the soul. 'God', says Ruysbroeck again, 'works this spiritual touching within us first, before all gifts; and yet it is known and tasted by us last of all. For only when we have sought God in love in all our practices, even to the inward deeps of our ground, do we first *feel* the inpouring of all the graces and gifts of God.'

These are the gifts, the habitudes, the characters, with which Infinite Spirit enhances Its finite and surrendered creature; expanding, pacifying and ennobling the narrow and unresting soul, and imparting to it a character which is deep and calm and selfless, like a share in a vast life. And all these are but the exercise or the effect of one love; poured out in the soul's very ground from Spirit to spirit, that it may return to Spirit again. For beyond all we can see, feel, think, or bear there ever awaits us

God, the Fact of all facts, perfect and complete. And the human soul, subject to succession, not perfect, not complete, finds its true life and full power only in an ever-growing surrender to that rich and living Reality.

VI

THE TWOFOLD LIFE

ONCE man has entered on this spiritual life, its growth if healthy will be not merely upwards but also outwards ; so that ever wider areas of interest and activity are included in its span and subdued to the supernatural demand. The gift of Wisdom, savouring God Transcendent, and aware of His touchings of the spirit, penetrates and enhances that gift of Understanding, which reads experience in the light of God Immanent, and the gift of Counsel, which subjects all personal choice to the secret counsellings of that Will in Whom all things are one. Thus all that is felt, done, loved and sacrificed is more and more perceived to be part of the apparatus through which Spirit Increate works on the spirit that is being created ; that by means of this created spirit's transformation, It may work on the whole fabric of life. Man, called to incarnate something of the Holy, must do it by a dedication of body as well as of soul ; purging and transforming the natural, and making it the vehicle of a supernatural life. This is the truth upon which the whole Christian religion is based : and the Pattern of that life as manifest among us

THE TWOFOLD LIFE

is marked above all by the rich variousness of its self-spending ardour, a ceaseless longing to teach, to heal, to save. Not our 'superior' faculties alone, our will and instinct for Eternity, but our 'lower' nature, our deeply-rooted correspondences with the created order, must be unselfed and harmonized to the purposes of the Spirit, and the unity of our being restored. For that being is called to be a bridge between temporal and eternal Reality. 'I will ask of God', said Elizabeth Leseur, 'such an enlargement of soul, that I may love Him with ardour, serve Him with joy, and transmit His radiance to the world.'

This sense of total surrender to Spirit for Its purposes and not our own, moving within the time-series as the agent of Unchanging Love, is the ruling characteristic of great saints, and the essence of Eternal Life. 'For as many as are led by the Spirit of God, *they* are the sons of God.' The first term of the spiritual life must always be God's hidden but felt Presence and action, His absolute priority; not the little soul He moves and incites to seek Him, still less that soul's interests, feelings, or experiences. And this hidden Presence, itself unchanging, discloses Itself in many ways and on many levels; from that which we call wholly natural, to that which, lying beyond our comprehension, we refer to the 'supernatural' world. So too the response that is asked from Its child and creature may involve the extreme of world-renouncement, or may seem to pin down the soul to the most homely duties of the natural level, and possess none of the characters we attribute to the contemplative life. Yet even so, lived towards God, based upon that ground where Spirit guides and sustains us, each response, whatever its appearance, will have the quality of prayer.

Thus we see that this life, in its perfect norm, can neither be a life of pure contemplation, nor a life of pure action. It must in its own small way enter that balanced rhythm of rapt communion and self-spending love which ruled the earthly life of Christ ; a life in which the soul expands to embrace and love and serve the greatest possible number of persons, contacts and events, and calls in its faculties to find again their meaning and their poise in God. And it is this double movement at its fullest, with all that it involves of tension and sacrifice, which constitutes the supernatural charity of saints. We, standing at the verge of their mysterious country, can only guess at the experiences which are contained in ' the breadth, and length, and depth, and height ' of this humbling yet exalting life in God. Indeed, when we consider the curve of St. Paul's life, the shattering events of his conversion, his total surrender and its results, we can hardly dare to suppose that our best thoughts penetrate far into the meaning of these words. Yet, in their own small way, our souls too are required to expand in more directions than one. Because our lives unfold in a world impregnated with God Immanent, the first movement of quickened spirit will be a

THE TWOFOLD LIFE

willing and supple self-giving to His purposes therein declared. On the other hand, because in the last resort He alone can suffice and complete us, we need a certain solitude and withdrawal from succession, in which to experience those interior ' stirrings and touchings ' of the Spirit which are the secret causes of the spiritual life. These movements must balance and enrich each other. Neither must be seized and enjoyed for its own sake alone. For we are being remade in order that we may be useful : not in order that we may abandon our post within that time-series where God acts, and wills to act, through human souls.

His Spirit comes to us, as Caussade said, in ' the sacrament of the present moment '. Joy and pain, drudgery and delight, humiliation and consolation, tension and peace—each of these contrasting experiences reaches us fully charged with God ; and does, or should incite us to an ever more complete self-giving to God. But each experience, as such, is neutral when seen only in natural regard. It is then merely part of that endless chain of cause and effect of which our temporal lives are made. It can only touch our deepest selves, help or hinder the growth of the spirit, in so far as we do or do not direct our wills through it in love and reverence to Him. There is only one life—the ' spiritual ' life consists in laying hold on it in a particular way ; so that action becomes charged with contemplation, and the Infinite is served in and through all finite things. The twofold experience of Spirit, as a deeply felt inward Presence and as the Ocean of reality and life, must be actualized in a twofold response of the soul: a response which is at once 'active' and 'contemplative', outgoing and indrawing, an adoring gaze on the Splendour over against us, and a humble loving movement towards the surrendered union of will and Will. 'Whenever the Lord is about to bestow grace on us', says Osuna, 'He says (at least equivalently) what was said to Rebecca: " Let us call the maid, and ask her will ".'

Thus total abasement before the transcendent Perfect is one side of the spiritual life. Adoption into the supernatural series—divine sonship, with its obligation of faithful service within the Divine order—is the other side. The Seraphim in Isaiah's vision, who veiled their faces before the unmeasured Glory, were yet part of the economy through which that Glory was poured out on the world: and the experience of reality which begins with the prophet's awe-struck vision and utter abasement before the Holy, ends on the words ' Send me! '

This double action of the soul, standing away from the Perfect in contemplation and seeking union with It in love, and this double consciousness of the Holy as both our Home and our Father, are the characters of a fully developed Christian spirituality. But these characters are not found in their classic completeness in any one individual. We only discern their balanced splendour in the corporate life of surrendered spirits; the Communion of Saints. Not the individual mystic in his solitude,

THE TWOFOLD LIFE

but the whole of that Mystical Body, in its ceaseless self-offering to God, is the unit of humanity in which we can find reflected the pattern of the spiritual life. And as regards the individual, the very essence of that life is contained in a docile acceptance of his own peculiar limitations and capacities, a loyal response to vocation—a response which, though it may sometimes be passive in appearance, is ever charged with the activity of God. 'I see no difference', said Bérulle, as he bade farewell to his brethren before setting forth upon an onerous mission, ' between those who go and those who stay at home. In one sense all are sent ; for there is a double mission, one interior and the other exterior. And it is on the interior mission of grace, of mercy, and of charity, that I declare all to be sent.'

So the life of spirit means such personal subordination to God's total action, as weaves into one the inward and outward movements of the soul ; and endues all work with contemplation, and makes of contemplation the most mortified and self-abandoned of all work. In this world, such a life must always involve a certain tension between the two movements, a nailing to the Cross of the restless will, and constant failures in adjustment and acceptance which keep the individual painfully aware of incompleteness, and ever open to the wholesome and purifying experience of penitence. Yet this tension, this acceptance of suffering and limitation is the price of all real life : every new entrance into the creative order, every union with Reality, however feeble and incomplete. No servant of truth or beauty, in art, exploration, science or thought, can escape the ascetic law. If our response to circumstance consists mainly in an unchecked yielding to the attractions and repulsions of sensitive nature, given over like a restless sea to ' the winds of pain and pleasure, hope and fear ', then we wholly miss the interior significance of that web of events in which we are placed, and which can at every point convey God.

So the deepening and enriching of man's Godward life by a regular and deliberate feeding of the theocentric temper, and the cleansing of that vision which beholds Him, are the indivisible implicits of spiritual growth. For the loving inclination of the purified will towards God alone makes possible the inflow of His feeding strengthening Spirit ; and that supersensual Food increases in its turn the energy, the purity, the self-abandoned meekness of the growing spirit's tendency to Him.

PURIFICATION

I

THE ESSENCE OF PURGATION

THERE is a type of sacred picture, very popular in the period of the Counter-Reformation, which shows a saint ascending to the foot of the Cross; and the Crucified stooping to His servant and by one arm drawing him to union with Himself. It is a symbolic representation of the *Anima Christi*; that double movement of desire and grace, which is the formula of the spiritual life. The steps on which the saint ascends to that share in the divine self-giving which is the fulfilment of joy, are variously regarded. St. Francis stands secure on the great unriven rock of perfect charity, and finds that he can reach his Master there. St. Ignatius climbs more gradually, by the successive steps of obedience, patience, humility and love. But it is the same arduous ascent and the same attainment, whatever the path which is taken by the soul. The Christian mystic conceives this pictorially, as a share in the Cross: the entry of the human spirit into the redemptive order of the Holy, achieved partly by its own deliberate upward struggle and partly by the generous stooping down of the Divine. And these two movements of created and Creative love are the causes of that double purification—at once active and passive—which is the condition of the soul's entry into, and persistence in, the spiritual life. 'Set love in order, thou that lovest Me.' And this setting in order of our undisciplined desires, this hard climb-up from the instinctive life of 'nature' to the transformed life of 'grace', could never be undertaken without a certain humble self-revelation of the Perfect, attracting to Itself our adoring love and awakening our sense of imperfection and our zest. All the apparatus of religion is meant to make us accessible to that revelation, and stimulate our response: in other words, to awaken and feed our charity.

'A man', says Ruysbroeck, 'should always, in all his works, stretch towards God with love; Whom, above all things, he aims at and loves.' But this requires the drastic elimination of all those desires and repulsions which side-track the will, and conflict with the total inclination of our personality towards God; and the deliberate direction of the great drive of our nature—its love and will, its passions and energies—to that supreme attraction and demand. Only thus can we achieve that entire fulfilment of the First Commandment which is the substance of a life of prayer. 'A soul enslaved by anything less than God', says St. John of the Cross, 'becomes by this fact incapable of

THE ESSENCE OF PURGATION

union with Him.' Though the life of the senses may seem the most obvious sphere of disorder, it is at a deeper level that the real purgation of self-love must take place. The soul, our total invisible being—with a range of experience and possibility stretching from a total response to the world of the senses to a total concentration on intellectual or spiritual good—is required to withdraw from its unreal correspondences, turn its emotional drive in a new direction, and subordinate its sacred powers of knowing and of loving to the overruling claim and invitation of Reality. All pouring out of will and desire towards lesser objects, unless Spirit remains the ultimate aim, breaks up the unity of the soul's life and wastes its powers. This stern truth, indeed, rules all levels of our existence; and requires of us the normal restraints of common sense, as well as the absolute self-stripping of sanctity.

Too often, the passive and active aspects of the one living and mysterious process of purification—the deep action of Spirit on spirit, at once attracting, penetrating and abasing us, and our deliberate costly effort of self-conquest and response—are treated as if they were distinct. But in reality they cannot be divided. Within the soul's actual life, it is impossible to separate with a sure hand the work of God from that of the surrendered will; whether in mortification or in prayer. It is true that the self's own action at first appears most vigorous and obvious, and then may seem to fade away. But this appearance is deceptive. From the very beginning, the active and passive adjustments of the spirit to the ever-deepening demands of the Holy go on simultaneously. The immanent Power works ceaselessly on the half-made creature; yet always by way of an incitement, a secret revision of standards, a stirring of love, which by turns attracts and shames us and calls forth our full power of response.

We are apt to think of 'mortification' as a codified moral discipline, imposed from without on the soul; whereas it really arises from the very character of the spiritual life, and is above all an evidence of growth. It is the name of those inevitable changes which the psyche must undergo, in the transfer of interest from self to God. Active purification represents the simple effort of our embryonic faith, hope and charity—three aspects and expressions of one state, or tendency to God, as realized by understanding will and heart—to capture and rule the house of the soul, and vanquish all hostile powers. Passive purification is best understood as a part of the Spirit's general creative action on us; given through circumstances and interior movements, and felt specially in the pressure of His demands on our innate self-will and self-love. 'It is one and the same flame of love', says St. John of the Cross, 'which will one day unite itself to the soul to glorify it, and which now invades it to purify it.' And whilst our own ascetic action, and a conviction of its reality and impor-

THE ESSENCE OF PURGATION 101

tance, is essential to our spiritual health, it is through this penetrating and rectifying action of Spirit, moving all things to their appointed end, and in all its operations gratefully received by us, that the real transformation of the soul is worked.

> Lava quod est sordidum,
> Riga quod est aridum,
> Sana quod est saucium.
>
> Flecte quod est rigidum,
> Fove quod est frigidum,
> Rege quod est devium.

We must think of the pressure and penetration of God, on and through His many-levelled living Universe, as steady and continuous. This discovery of the ceaseless Divine action, perhaps the most crucial experience of life, is the clue to the mysterious facts of purification and prayer. Once recognized and trusted, it emancipates us from all slavery to particular methods and guides. We now realize ourselves to be directly moved and led by Spirit ; always equally sanctifying, whether its cleansing action reach us by outward events, duty, suffering, mental life, or prayer. We, at each point, are more or less susceptible to that purifying action, according to the way in which we use our limited freedom ; our capacity for docility, effort, suffering and love. This susceptibility will normally be manifested in our response to the stimulus of events ; and more profoundly, in the movements of the soul in prayer. The bracing, bending, softening and reordering which the alertly loving spirit then desires and asks, are commonly given to it through the homely frictions and demands of daily life ; sweetened and sanctified, because through and in them are discerned the personal touch and Presence of the Spirit, Who alone knows the path of every creature and is for that creature at once Way, Truth and Life.

So it is, that there is no parity whatever between the intensity of those external, or even internal trials which discipline us, and their purifying result. The dripping tap or barking dog which teaches patience is as much an instrument of God as the shattering blow which tears two souls apart. A soul in the sphere of purification may receive the maximum of suffering—and, if abandoned to God, the maximum of cleansing—through an apparently inadequate event ; if the response which that event demands be of such a nature as to mortify the root of self-regard. Even the outward incidents of the Passion were not proportioned to the dread suffering and victory of which they were the proximate cause. One and the same event may be charged for this soul with the purifying call to an utter self-abandonment ; and merely incite that soul to a sterile resentment. The cleansing and transforming power of suffering abides not in the degree of pain experienced, but in the degree of acceptance achieved ; the *Fiat voluntas tua* with which the soul meets the action of God-Spirit in and through events.

THE ESSENCE OF PURGATION

Thus we see that the common notion of the 'purgative way' as merely the equivalent of moral self-conquest, is not adequate to the deep facts of the spiritual life. Though it is true that the opening phase of that life will commonly involve direct conflict with obvious faults, the real purification of the soul is not an unpleasant experience of limited duration—a drastic supernatural 'cure'—to which we must submit ourselves in order to be 'disinfected of egoism', and released from the tyranny of the instinctive life. Those who prefer the neatness of the museum label to the disconcerting actuality of the living soul, always tend to describe as successive experiences which are really simultaneous; and sometimes they become the dupes of their own tidiness. They like to arrange the inner life in a series of stages, each to be completed and left behind. But this convenient diagram has only a symbolic relation to the real facts. That strange necessity of love which we know and experience within the time-series as 'purification', is really an effect of the eternal action of the Divine Charity; reaching and touching our souls through events. That touch and action must mean suffering, till our disharmony with God is done away; but takes an ever more subtle and interior form as our life develops, and its centre of interest passes from the sensible to the intellectual, and at last to the spiritual sphere. Thus the purifying demand seems to us to proceed step by step with the growth of that life ; till the whole of the intellectual and spiritual being, no less than the instinctive nature, is simplified, cleansed of self-interest, and transformed in God.

Moreover, as the growing spirit comes to realize this process as an essential and permanent strand in its true life, so its own acts of humble and loving correspondence, its secret renunciations and faithful acceptance, will grow in purity and depth. Then the very discipline of purification becomes a means of communion, and deepens into prayer ; more and more laying open the soul to the flood of the Spirit's unmeasured life. For the purifying worth of prayer consists in the increasing contrast which it sets up between the holy God and the creature ; subordinating that creature's fugitive activities and desires to the standard set by this solemn apprehension of Reality. Hence in practice, prayer or attention to God, and purification or self-adjustment to and with Him, must proceed together. Prayer tends directly to God ; mortification removes the de-ordination of desire, and concentrates our will and love on Him alone. These are the two completing aspects of one undivided life ; and if we think of them separately, it is merely for the sake of convenience.

This twofold progress, to and in God, is what St. John of the Cross means by the ' ascent of Mount Carmel '. And Mount Carmel is like one of those mountains which have many summits ; so that each

THE ESSENCE OF PURGATION

time we think we have reached our limit, we see a new height beyond us, more beautiful and more absolute in its demand; and again the glimmering Presence, the same yet ever-changing, beckons us on. Two by-paths accompany and constantly entice the mountaineer. One offers the natural life in all its fullness and charm; the other offers spiritual consolations and experiences. Both are to be avoided by the instructed climber: for at best they lead to the pleasant lower pastures of faith. The ascent to which he has been called is to the unseen summits of the Spirit; and that means the narrow way, the rock, the rope, the guide, and such a denudation of all preference and comfort, all softness, unreality and excess, as leaves him at last capable of giving all that Spirit asks, and receiving all that Spirit gives.

First the field of normal consciousness and conduct, where the 'I' lives in contact with the world of sense, and under the constant stimulus of desire, must be submitted to the purifying power; reordered in accordance with the standards of reality. Next the intellectual region, where the mind is always at work analysing and interpreting, must subordinate the separate findings of reason to the overwhelming certitudes of faith; and the psychic world of memory and imagination in which so much of our waking life is passed, must disclose its fugitive and approximate character over against God. Last, the will, the principle of action, and the very expression of our personal love and life, is to be cleansed of self-interest by the action of Divine Love ; that the whole unified being 're-formed' in faith, hope and charity, may tend to its one objective, the incomprehensible Being of God.

II

THE CLEANSING OF THE SENSES

THE notion that the world in which we find ourselves is really very nice, and that those impressions of the dread reality and penetrative power of sin which haunt awakened spirits, are merely due to ignorance, atavism or ill-adjustment, is not truly adequate to the facts of our situation. It has never satisfied mature souls. The saints, whose whole lives consist in a loyal and delighted response to God Present, are seldom easy-going optimists. Their humble steady consciousness of the reality of Spirit seems to bring a compensating sense of the real dangers among which we live ; and of great spiritual energies which are hostile to the attainment of God. Christ never represented salvation as something to be attained easily. Few, He thought, find the steep and narrow path which leads away from the ever-burning rubbish dump, and towards the austere victory of the Cross. Many are called, few chosen. Those who seem first, are often last. This is a strand in His teaching which we prefer to minimize or forget ; but it stares at us from the Gospels, and is endorsed by the experience of the soul. The ancient prayer of the Church for the souls of the dead, sums up her consciousness of those possibilities other than beatitude which always wait for our unstable human personality, and may snatch their victory even at the very end: as if, emerging from bodily life, yet charged with all the dispositions it had fostered, an awful choice of direction did really lie before each spirit. *Libera eas* from the mouth of the lion, from all the untamed violence latent in life, the devouring element; that they may not sink with the decay of nature into the deep lake of darkness, never to emerge again. *Ne absorbeat eas tartarus, ne cadant in obscurum.*

And this choice, this risk, vividly felt in that decisive moment, recurs at every stage of the interior life; which is constantly solicited from those two directions which we roughly distinguish as the spheres of sense and of spirit, of nature and of grace. For the soul, as St. Teresa saw, is one and indivisible. It is the whole invisible reality of our being; the immaterial self which informs and uses the total mechanism of body and mind, and by means of that mechanism responds to the various attractions and demands of our mixed environment. And the question for man is, where shall the centre of its energies be placed? In that vigorous, instinctive life we share with the animals; which is rooted in the time-series, and totally concerned with the satisfaction of desire and the maintaining of our foothold in the physical world? Or in that 'fine point of the spirit' which is turned towards God and craves for God? The problem is not to be solved by the mere

THE CLEANSING OF THE SENSES

rejection or repression of 'sensitive nature'; for there is no watertight bulkhead between the sensitive and spiritual levels of the soul. It is an aspect of our amphibious situation, that one part of our being can never be purified apart from the other. They flow into and affect one another. There is no desire which belongs so entirely to the senses that it leaves the spirit untouched; whilst in the best and purest of our supposed 'spiritual' experiences, there is always some admixture of sense. Even our final beatitude is held by Christian theology to depend somehow on the continued possession of 'body' as well as 'soul'.

So our biological inheritance must be the first matter of purification, because it cannot be left behind without tearing our very selves in two. The great energies of 'nature' must be transformed and brought into line, if human personality is fully to serve the purposes of 'grace'. Hence the conflict which is an inevitable part of all spiritual growth. For the deepest soul, the most interior self, since it is spirit, must always when awakened say to the indwelling and enveloping Presence which is creating it—' Strip me, scourge me, cleanse me, take me and subdue me to Thy purpose. Lo! I come to do Thy will.' Indeed, there is nothing else for it to do. It achieves its fullest life by an utter self loss: at these deep levels, where Spirit and spirit meet, sacrifice and ecstasy are one. When we remember our real situation, our entire and child-like dependence on the Spirit of God penetrating and

THE GOLDEN SEQUENCE

supporting us, and the centrality of this relation for our whole existence : then, the enslavement of will and emotion to anything that deflects or impairs the purity of this unceasing correspondence with God, is seen to cripple our true lives, and twist our souls out of shape. And the unmortified, unchecked response of will and feeling to the attraction of any objective which is less than God does this.

But sensitive nature, in and through which the spirit must support itself in the time-series, and there receive and manifest the Divine Action, rebels against this austere demand for the ordering of its love. It desires its own satisfactions, clings to its own universe, plays for its own hand. Even when the crude egoistic impulses to self-assertion and greed have been subdued upon the physical level—those acquisitive, lustful, combative tempers which the race carries forward as untransformed energy from its sub-human past—they merely transfer their energies to the spiritual sphere. A selfish, greedy and acquisitive attitude towards the attractions of spirit replaces a selfish, greedy and acquisitive attitude towards the attractions of sense. Spiritual pride, spiritual envy, and spiritual gluttony are not less hostile to God than their carnal counterparts ; for they mean that the soul's true life is still turned inwards on itself. The stain of self-interest lies on its prayer and dries up its adoration, the poison of spiritual egoism saps its health. And only the purging action of Spirit, humbly asked and bravely endured, can set this situation right.

THE CLEANSING OF THE SENSES

Lava quod est sordidum,
Riga quod est aridum,
Sana quod est saucium.

Thus one and the same law of tranquil self-oblivion must be applied to the whole house of the soul ; not only to the lower story, but to the upper as well—that region of spiritual desire, where our secret self-love so often finds a lair. For only in the tranquillity which is achieved by the death of all personal demand can the delicate impulsions of the Spirit be discerned. And this we can only win by turning the whole of our instinctive life in a new direction, away from self-fulfilment however noble, and towards entire self-mergence in God ; setting its vigorous love in order, giving it without reserve to the purposes of the Will. Here psychology and religion go hand in hand. Each recommends the drastic re-ordering and sublimation of desire, its redemption from self-interest, as the pathway to interior peace : and this redeeming of desire contains in itself that whole purification of the sensitive life, which St. John of the Cross calls the first of the three nights through which the Godward tending soul is called to pass. First on the natural level and then on the spiritual level, ' appetite ' in the sense of undisciplined and egoistic choice must be renounced. For all the scattered cravings, illusory ambitions and emotional inclinations of the ' I ' represent so much energy subtracted, so much interest deflected, from the great drive of the ' Me ' towards God.

Thus it sometimes seems as though the whole life

of faith were contained in the continual battle with our instinctive desire for personal satisfactions, possessions or success, material, emotional, and spiritual : that a ceaseless *agere contra* must be the law of spiritual growth. But things are not really quite so grim as this. From another angle, the life of the spirit is seen to consist on one hand in its active loving movement—often checked and baffled but faithfully renewed—towards an ever-closer correspondence with achieved Perfection : on the other, in the ceaseless purifying action of the Divine Life present in circumstance upon our unstable and unfinished being, and the soul's humble, grateful and passive acceptance of this. As the souls in the *Purgatorio* ran eagerly to the cleansing Mountain, and climbed from terrace to terrace, not urged by God's justice but drawn by His love ; so vigorous effort is one side of the purifying process, but only one side —it is a preparation of the matter of the sacrament. The essential change is worked, we know not how, by the cleansing action of the Spirit working in the hidden deeps, bending the rigid will to suppleness and melting the ice about the frozen heart. For the goal to which our spirits move is that life-giving state of active union in which, knowing that we abide in God, we are really at home ; feeding on Him, are satisfied ; and lost in Him, fulfil our life.

There is a marvellous moment at the end of the *Purgatorio*, in which a tremor passes through the Holy Mountain ; and all the souls on all the terraces, forgetting their own pains, rise to their feet

THE CLEANSING OF THE SENSES

in joy and sing the *Gloria*. And when Dante asks what has happened, he is told that one soul, casting off the last fetters of selfish desire, has risen and gone forward in freedom to God. In that one act, which turns the whole of the self's will towards the Universal Will, purification is complete. But so tough are the attachments of the senses, so inveterate is the creature's frenzied clutch on fugitive possessions and delights, that many minor operations are necessary before all the adhesions are cleared away.

Thus it follows that everything must go from the soul in whom the thirst for God has been awakened which competes with the one overruling attraction of Spirit. All clutch and grab, ill-will and turbulence ; all those primitive exhausting passions and absorbing childish ambitions, all the vestigial relics of the cave and jungle, which civilized society disguises but does not suppress. But the purity which is to be achieved is not the sterile safety of something that is kept in the refrigerator. Within Spirit's sphere of influence, and capable of its transforming power, there is offered to the soul an infinity of lesser generous loves. The over-ruling Love of God in its quickening and penetrating beauty will give all these a certain purifying and sacrificial character ; purging them of violence and self-regard, and replacing the concentrated fevers of desire by the generous glow of a wide-spreading charity. 'When we are masters of ourselves', says Gerlac Petersen, ' our footsteps will not be straitened ; but freely and liberally shall we walk with our Lord, looking at all things with Him.' This is the formula of that sanctity—at once so divine and so human—which makes of human personality, in all its richness and emotional beauty, a channel of the Love of God.

And it is surely just because the senses are so mysterious and so holy, that these senses must be cleansed, re-ordered and unselfed. We cannot, in fact, really split ourselves up into 'sensual' and 'spiritual' man; but in all our varied power of love and suffering, must accept the contributions and the limitations of sense. The Christian cannot avoid the fact that he finds himself within a sacramental order; and cannot correspond with that sacramental order on the level of spirit alone. Sense must intervene in our responses to reality; and cannot, unless docile to the over-ruling Spirit and purged of the infection of desire. This means a steady and courageous shifting of the soul's centre of action from the circumference inwards to its true centre, the deep where it abides in God; and thence a rich and selfless expansion, which is the reward of that preliminary stripping and retreat. Thus it is not a harsh dualism but a profound incarnationalism which requires us to set in order our physical and emotional life, and subordinate all vagrant longings to the single passion for God. 'A heart filled with desires', says St. John of the Cross, ' knows nothing of liberty.'

III

THE CLEANSING OF THE INTELLECT

ST. JOHN OF THE CROSS describes three 'nights', three kinds and degrees of obscurity, which the growing spirit must experience during its transition from that natural life within which we all emerge, and to which we are adjusted, to the other life which is 'transformed in God'. He says that these nights are like the strong soap and soda which cleanse us from all the stains of unreality, and restore us to the purity in which we can receive the divine light. This symbolism at first repels us by its apparent harshness; its purely negative character. But when we examine it, we see that it is a desperate attempt to describe the sequence of psychological states through which our limited consciousness does and must move, from its normal whole-hearted acceptance of that unquestioned world of 'common sense' which is shown to us by the senses, to correspondence with that other level of reality, dimly yet most truly known in our ascents to the soul's apex—a world which is ever 'dark to the intellect, though radiant to the heart'.

For the three 'nights' of St. John are really the successive phases of one undivided process; the disconcerting and purifying discovery of the mystery, the cloud of unknowing, which wraps us round. They are like the increasing dark through which the earth turns so gravely and quietly from one day to the next. The soul moves in them from dusk to full night ; and thence to that luminous darkness which precedes the dawn, and has in it a tenderness and wonder, a quality of revelation, unknown to the ' good visibility ' of the average day. When prayer first brings us into this twilight of the spirit, the sharply defined landscape within which we have been accustomed to arrange our religious experiences, and all the certitudes and satisfactions, religious and other, mediated by the senses, lose their familiar colour, importance and shape. They become less solid and certain ; more mysterious. As the bright field and the safe homely creatures, which in daylight we took easily for granted, assume an alien and primeval majesty, reveal something of their inward being, at the first approach of night ; so it is when the dusk of the spirit falls on the familiar religious scene. The crisp ' facts ' of an organized faith suffer a strange transformation. They loom up at us, dim, huge, half-realized, and yet more deeply living than before ; like forest trees before the rising of the moon. And now we begin to be aware of their infinite solemnity and significance, their treasures of hidden truth and beauty ; and of our ignorance in respect of their real meaning, our shallowness of comprehension over against their depth. The world of religion is no longer a concrete fact proposed for

THE CLEANSING OF THE INTELLECT 117

our acceptance and adoration. It is an unfathomable universe which engulfs us, and which lives its own majestic uncomprehended life: and we discover that our careful maps and cherished definitions bear little relation to its unmeasured reality.

' O Lord my God,' cries Nicholas of Cusa, ' I behold thee in the entrance of Paradise and I know not what I see, for I see naught visible. This alone I know, that I know not what I see and never can know. . . . Thou, God, who art Infinity, canst only be approached by him whose intellect is in ignorance ; to wit, by him who knows himself to be ignorant of Thee.'

How purifying, how deeply humbling is this discipline of ignorance ; this sense of the great life that enfolds us, the dim country surrounding and underlying the small bright patch to which alone our analytic minds are adequate. ' For of all other creatures and their works ', says *The Cloud of Unknowing*, ' may a man through grace have fulness of knowing, and well can he think of them. But of God Himself can no man think. And therefore I would leave all that thing that I can think, and choose to my love that thing that I cannot think.'

The soul that has received this intimation of the true relation between its small perceptions and the universe of Spirit, has experienced once for all the essence of that purgation of the understanding which prepares the way of faith. For what matters here is that the mind shall become so quietly limpid, so clear of its own deceptive notions and discriminations, that it receives simply and humbly the subtle touch of God; 'understanding because it does not seek to understand',—as we understand the mystery of the night. Then we realize that prayer only achieves depth and substance when it passes beyond and above our intelligence; and we know not what we do, because our action is engulfed in the mighty act of Spirit, and we are for the time being lost in the night of God.

Entering this 'night of faith' which is to purge the mind of all its intellectual pride and self-assurance, the soul at first feels utterly lost. Sensitive nature is deprived of the accustomed support which it has received from visible religion; and reason receives its first daunting revelation of that overplus of Reality with which it can never deal. The miracle-play is over, the foot-lights have gone out, and we must go home under the stars. Their radiance seems very dim after the theatre lights. But only with our docile acceptance of this enfolding darkness can we escape from the imaginary world of sensitive nature and learn to centre our being on God alone. This strips the understanding, the memory and the will of all fantasy, all easy self-assurance, and forces them to face the dark reality of Spirit and the narrow limits of our possible experience. 'The soul does not unite itself to God in this world by understanding, by enjoying, by imagining, nor by any faculty of sensitive nature',

THE CLEANSING OF THE INTELLECT

says St. John of the Cross ; but by the generous act of trust which turns from all these props to a bare adherence in faith ' free, naked, pure and simple without mode or manner '.

' God is greater than our heart.' But all that this means for the soul which tends to Him cannot be learnt without a painful cleansing of the intellectual life. For it requires us to refuse all trust in the final worth of our separate and distinct experiences— in the workings of philosophic reason on one hand, or of religious imagination on the other—while accepting the intimations of God conveyed by these imperfect instruments. This is the ' divine ignorance ' which cleanses the interior mirror and stills the restless mind, in order that it may receive in humble tranquillity the impress of Spirit. And purification here means the steady refusal to pour ourselves out towards the merely attractive and consoling, or the dangerously clear ; the discarding of easy diagrams and clever explanations of the Invisible, the feeding of our humble sense of mystery. It means accepting our ignorance, acknowledging the awful gap between the Creator and the creature, and refusing to narrow-down Reality to our own small apprehensions and desires. All concepts of God, from the most crude to the most ' spiritual ', fall to silence before His face. And it is the confession— indeed the joyful acceptance—of this ignorance, whether realized by way of ' pure faith ' or ' pure love ', which is the essence of the mind's active purification ; preparing it for that deeper and more searching action of Spirit which is called the passive night of the soul.

Being what we are, and living as we do a disorderly and restless life of ceaseless confusion between the fugitive and enduring, rational and instinctive levels, and vagrant correspondences with this and that, we can hardly hope to come to any real apprehension of Spirit without such a deep and painful purgation of the mind. Here we are not concerned with disorders of the moral life, or conflicts between ' higher ' and ' lower ' desires : but with a total reconditioning, expansion and unselfing of the intelligence, so that it may respond by a simple movement of faith and love to an environment of which Spirit, with its mysterious demands and attractions, is the ruling fact.

Flecte quod est rigidum.

When our first crude interpretation of life according to the witness of sense and suggestions of personal desire is transcended, our further and more dangerous claim to interpret Reality in its depth and richness by means of those ' rational principles ' to which we have attained, must be transcended too ; if the intellect is ever to become cleansed of pride, docile to mystery, and accept the limitations within which it can safely work. Since the reality of Spirit cannot possibly be clear to our sense-conditioned understanding, all vivid definition, all appearance of logic and clarity, all attempts to equate ' religion ' with ' science ' and make the natural and super-

THE CLEANSING OF THE INTELLECT

natural fit, are deceptive. For that which is adequate to us can never be adequate to God ; nor could a Reality we were able to understand ever quench our transcendental thirst. We have to recognize our intellectual concepts as the useful makeshifts which they really are ; paper currency which permits the circulation of spiritual wealth, but must never be mistaken for gold.

For there is no correspondence, no parity, between our most admirable notions and the Being of God ; and we only begin to approach a certain obscure knowledge of His presence, when we consent to abandon our arrogant attempts towards definition and understanding, become the meek recipients of His given lights, and the silent worshippers of His unfathomable Reality. Only by a movement of bare faith does the mind really draw near to Him. This, in the last resort, is all it can do here : pacifying the soul's house, gathering in its scattered interests, passions, desires and spiritual preferences, and subduing them to the single fact of God. Yet this is not to mean a mere wholesale ejection from our mental life and our religious practice of all that is not ' purely spiritual '. Real life is richer and more difficult than this. We are called to a just and disinterested use of that many-levelled world which surrounds us with its graded realities, and in which we are to find and love—beyond all other objects of desire—the one full Reality, all-penetrating Spirit ; the Origin and sustainer of all these lesser lives, lights and loves.

So the purification of intellect does not mean the deliberate cultivation of a holy stupidity, nor yet a wholesale retreat from the sensible and the homely : for then we reject the rich ore in which the treasure is hidden, and abandon the only machinery for dealing with it that we possess. It is as human beings, transformed but none the less completely human, that our life toward Spirit must be lived ; and within the sensible order to which we are adjusted that we must receive the touch of God. Therefore we shall need the perpetual intervention of the senses, conveying the messages of Spirit ; and in order to deal with those messages, the best mental patterns and concepts that we can achieve. But if these are not to delude us, we shall need also a constant, humble remembrance of their proximate and symbolic nature ; an awe-struck recognition of the over-plus, the solemn mystery which penetrates and sustains our finite world ; a one-sided relation to the Reality of God. We must never confuse with Him any gift or experience of the contingent world ; even though we are seldom able to approach Him in isolation from all sensible signs, or distinguish with certainty substance from accident.

And this is where the stress and difficulty of our mental purgation is most deeply felt. It creates for us a situation which is at once costly, humbling and bracing. It asks a ceaseless tension, a childlike acceptance of the Infinite given to us in and with the finite ; which both redeems us from the risk of mere quietism, and protects us from intellectual pride,

THE CLEANSING OF THE INTELLECT 123

the arrogant claim to ' know ' God. The purifying action drives the soul's centre of action inwards from the circumference to the real ground of its life, where Spirit indwells us ; but this withdrawal is balanced by a rich and selfless expansion, a generous outward movement which is the fruit of that preliminary stripping and retreat. The mind is cleansed, quietened and expanded, stops its restless effort to make things fit ; is opened to the ceaseless gentle action of the Spirit, which keeps us ever aware that the best of our apparent discoveries and experiences are crumbs with which God feeds us from the infinite storehouse of Truth. Here then the soul's attitude must be undemanding and all-accepting : content to receive Spirit's revelation through earthly forms and figures, to gaze on the Cross and know that it offers us a truth we cannot fathom ; without disturbing reflections as to the aspect under which that truth is given in ' Orion or the Bear '.

So our aim must be to escape from all confusion of gift with Giver ; from anything which deflects the soul's upward and outward look to That beyond itself which it desires. For the pure radiance of God, says St. John, is never absent from the soul ; but the images and concepts with which our understandings are filled, and to which we attribute reality, prevent its diffusion. And the first of these impediments is that tendency to identify sensible signs and spiritual things, which has always haunted the history of religion. For here Man is called upon to accept the humbling necessity of his mixed nature, and receive news of the Spirit through the channels of sense ; yet ever to practise a careful discrimination between the revealing medium and the Reality revealed. To remember that in religion all demand for the sharp and clear, all trust in the image, and satisfaction with the image, is unsafe ; whilst refusing the attractive temptation to abandon the whole world of image and thought, and sink into a mere undifferentiated 'awareness' of Spirit—this indeed purifies the understanding and subordinates it to mystery, but does not annihilate it. For then, refusing to attach ourselves to anything we are able to know and comprehend, we go out with intense desire through and in these known and familiar signs, to That which is inaccessible to the mind ; and through that which we taste and feel, touch That which transcends all taste and all feeling.

Once the sensible world, both natural and religious, has become truly sacramental, it has become safe. Then, holding together its essential holiness and its pathetic failures, and reaching out through both in naked faith to God, the mind is released from slavery to its own conceptual system ; and preserved from mistaking signs for things, pictures for portraits, and even the most impressive movements and satisfactions of the religious imagination for revelations of Reality. The spiritual life, so deep, free and elastic, so humble in its simplicity and so august in its span, is ruled by the undemanding adoration of that Reality. Thus it tends to such a simplification of our whole psychic nature, that faith, hope and

THE CLEANSING OF THE INTELLECT

charity—the supernatural vision trust and love—become the varying moods and colours of one single state ; a pure abandonment to the vast action of God.

So the soul in whom this life has been set going must subordinate all thoughts, concepts, insights, to this Divine action ; must cling to no religious image, nor claim for it absolute worth. On the other hand, entrance into this night of faith solves many of the difficulties of visible religion for us. Humbly acknowledging the entire ' otherness ' of Spirit and yet its gentle and continuous action within the world of sense, we can accept the most homely symbol and most absurd devotion for that which they are : modes of the self-giving of that Spirit which is modeless, yet which uses these sensible channels as a merciful condescension to our childish state, and manifests the royalty of love by meeting us on our own ground.

It will be seen from all this that the cleansing of the understanding must be achieved at least as much through prayer as through thought. Indeed, from beginning to end these work together in the soul. Here, as in the purifying of the natural life, all is contained in the humble tendency to God, and self-opening to His dark radiance. For this, of itself, plunges the spirit into that night of faith which can alone clear the mind of those unreal rationalisms, and those deceptive constructions, behind which we try to shelter from the simple and all-penetrating blaze of the Divine.

IV

MEMORY AND IMAGINATION

THE alert understanding, responding at all points to its environment, and always ready to interpret in accordance with its own diagrams and notions the messages which it receives, is yet only one part or aspect of that total psychic life which must be submitted to the purifying action of prayer. Great tracts of mental territory remain, which need to be cleansed from egoism, and redeemed from unreality, if all the powers of the self are to be ' gathered into the unity of the Spirit ' and transformed into a single instrument ; supple to the incitements and demands of God.

If our ' reasonable power ' of knowing, analysing and conceiving was required to acknowledge its own limitations over against the Infinite, and accept that humbling discipline of ignorance which is the foundation of faith ; still more, our mental stock in trade, all that mixed material of apperception which we use without ceasing—and mostly without thinking—in the ordinary business of everyday life, must be exposed to the cleansing rays of supersensual truth.

Lava quod est sordidum.

MEMORY AND IMAGINATION 127

That psychic storehouse, with its accumulation of remembered experience—pains and pleasures, repulsions and attractions, images and notions—colours all our reactions to reality, and enchains us to our past. Still more disastrous is the constant presence and penetrating odour of the psychic rubbish-heap; with its smouldering resentments, griefs and cravings, the empty shells that once held living passions, the tight hard balls of prejudice, the devitalizing regrets. All this ceaselessly tempts us to a sterile self-occupation, destructive of that simplicity which is the condition of a self-abandoned love. It reminds us of past sensible and emotional experiences, brings back into consciousness the old wounds to our self-love, old conflicts born of pride, anger, or self-will, and throws up distracting images whenever our minds are quiet.

Especially on our life towards Spirit, the insistent presence of this great well of memories, inclinations, images and dreams, exercises a constant and damaging influence : chaining us to the time-series, and giving past events, griefs and loves an immortal power. For here, God only must be sought, in and for Himself, in a pure and trustful streaming out of will and desire, a single undemanding flight ; without the backward glance towards anything already known, relinquished, longed for, or possessed. This entirely confident casting of the little spirit on the great Spirit of God, as birds on the supporting air—in spite of all the drag of the past, and suggestions of the untrustful mind—is that which theology means by the state of Hope. By it the memory whether of sins, fears or sorrows, is purified and sweetened. It is the soul's growing point, and the very means of its self-anchoring in God.

> La petite Espérance
> Est celle qui toujours commence.

The Bible is drenched in this spirit of unconquered Hope, a strange, other-worldly certitude shining through hours of destruction and grief; the upward confident look, out of the confused misery of human existence, towards an unfailing Power. In the Psalms which the Church recites on the days that lead to the Passion, the exquisite paradox of Hope achieved in suffering mounts up to its completion in the Cross. For only suffering can give this mysterious Hope to the spirit, teach it to throw the whole weight of its trust forwards upon God. ' Thou art my strong rock and my castle : be thou also my guide and lead me for thy Name's sake.'

It is not only the dreadful pull of self-occupation, the ingrained tendency of the psyche to turn backwards, rummage among its hoarded experiences, and reflect upon its own ideas, which deflects the undivided movement of the spirit towards God. The uncleansed memory operates disastrously within the very sanctuary of the devotional life. The total uncriticized content of our religious store-cupboard—all its phrases, images and symbols—entering into our apperceptive mass, brings many confusions in its train. We easily become the dupes of our own

MEMORY AND IMAGINATION

imaginative and psychological processes (and much of that which passes for 'religious experience' falls under this head); taking that which is less than Spirit for a direct intimation of the spaceless and eternal God. Thus we are led to suppose that we know Him, when as a matter of fact we only know our own ideas and feelings about Him; and content ourselves with turning over these unworthy notions and pictures of an unpicturable Reality.

The whole of popular religious art, and much religious literature too, witnesses to the deplorable result of identifying our dim yet deep intuition of God with its sensible embodiments; and to the fact that many so-called 'theological problems' really arise from the confusion of our imaginative machinery with that which it mediates. On the other hand, in the dangerous realm of supposed 'mystical' experience—which is most often psycho-sensual experience—the confusion of religious fantasy with religious fact is one of the most common traps awaiting fervent souls. The masters of prayer are untiring in their warnings upon this subject; and indeed any real apprehension of God's action, however faint and obscure, must sweep from the mind all images and all notions, and bring it to a state of pure receptivity. Nevertheless the lives of the saints, and of many who are far less than saints, are full of holy, poignant, or attractive day-dreams, projected images, interior conversations; which are the clear product of memory and imagination, but accepted without criticism as direct revelations of the supernatural world. Even so deeply spiritual a work as the *Revelations* of Julian of Norwich shows the influence of religious imagination on every page.

Thus it is of first importance to realize at once the uses, the limitations, and the dangers of this strange imaginative power, so little understood by us, which intervenes between our normal earthly experience and the simple contacts of the spiritual life. Most difficulties of adjustment between visible and invisible religion are caused by this confusion between our remembered images of God, and His unmediated presence revealed in prayer. What is here required is not an inhuman expulsion of all image, but a careful recognition of the true character of our religious furniture ; and a simplifying—so far as is possible without real impoverishment—of the interior decorations of the soul. The religious mind is often like a mid-Victorian drawing-room ; full of photographs, souvenirs, mirrors, superfluous draperies and bits of cabinet-work, which merely witness to our *bourgeois* fear of emptiness, and tend to develop in us a spiritual class consciousness, which colours our whole outlook on Reality. ' It is deplorable ', says Malaval, ' that among Christians there is often more of what one might call images and representations of piety, than the spirit of faith which ought to live in them. We always want to love and adore by figures, without going to the substance of things, and we stop at the means without going to the end.'

MEMORY AND IMAGINATION 131

Thus a clearing-up of the imaginative levels of religion is an essential and difficult part of the purification of our interior life. For here, in this stock-pot of the soul, primitive symbols, ancestral memories, pagan fantasies, and natural cravings decently disguised by the vestments of faith, all simmer together with the most sacred facts, figures and phrases: and when their confused results, coloured with emotion, emerge into consciousness, they are constantly accepted as 'religious experience'. Especially is this setting in order of the psychic storehouse, and understanding of its true nature, needed for any safe and fruitful use of image and meditation in the earlier degrees of prayer. For the haunting beauty of Christianity abides in the tension and contrast between the Absolute God and His self-revelation among men; the stooping-down of the Infinite to enter into finite forms. Thus the imaginative contemplation of these scenes through which Spirit is most richly revealed to us—and especially the mysteries of the earthly life of Christ—has always formed a valuable part of the education and purgation of the Christian consciousness. For here Spirit takes our mental apparatus and teaches through it. '*Mira! mira!*—Look! look!' cried St. Ignatius, as he led his pupils through those searching exercises which should bring them at last to the contemplation of the Love of God. And yet, that at which we look in awe and devotion, is at least in great part a work of memory and imagination; through which the riches of the

Spirit enter our field of perception, and are apprehended by our little souls. 'After all', says Malaval again, 'the body one imagines to oneself is not that of Our Lord; it is an imaginary body, which is as different in the imagination of each one, as the different imaginations of each one who conjures up the picture.' But so long as we recognize our secret theatre for that which it really is, and do not confuse the dramatic representation with the unearthly poem that it conveys, we are safe.

So, whilst the absolute character of the contrast between the Being of God and the imaginative embodiments of men (however beautiful and holy) must never be lost by us; yet here the arrogant and total rejection of the helps of the imagination and the senses is an equally dangerous excess. Each soul must discover and control the degree of its own dependence on the sensible: and, committed as we are to the mixed life of sense and spirit, none of us can strip our house of all its superfluous ornaments without threatening its hidden structure as well. The purification we are asked for is at once more difficult and less drastic than this. For Spirit, God, the substance of that which the soul loves and longs for, is ever conveyed within the image, form or figure that we contemplate; since He penetrates all life. And that part of prayer which matters most is the simple movement of the soul towards Him, adherence in her ground. That this most subtle encounter should be evoked, expressed and enmeshed within sensible forms is a

MEMORY AND IMAGINATION 133

humbling necessity of our being; and would do nothing but good to us, did we not tend to spoil everything by allowing sensitive nature to enter into such active relation with the outward sign, instead of waiting silently and faithfully on the inward grace.

That which we are called upon to do, is to distinguish as clearly as we may between the easy device of resting in quasi-sensible religious consolations or conceptions, and humble, unconsoled, self-naughting before God. We are to lean out towards Him in a simple act of total confidence, without pondering or analysing our 'experiences'; none of which are worth the act of self-abandoned faith in which we renounce them. As regards all such distinct religious images or conceptions, we must enter the 'cloud of forgetting', acknowledging their approximate and imaginary character and passing beyond them to a meek self-loss in God. Bathed in mystery as we are, we easily take refuge in the apparent and the attractive, and avoid the stern discipline of ignorance. But ' the more we withdraw from images and figures', says St. John of the Cross, ' the nearer we draw to God, Who has neither image, form, nor figure.' And though, literally interpreted, this saying might seem to shut the door on all visible and sacramental religion, it remains true if we remember that the saint is really reminding us of the ever-present danger of accepting sign instead of thing. We achieve the true liberty of detachment here, as in the instinctive life, by a plain recognition of imagination and memory as servants but never revealers of Truth. Through their disciplined use, the touch of God may be realized by us; and our sense of the supernatural deepened and enriched. Therefore the pure and supple mind will receive with simplicity all that God-Spirit gives to it by these strange channels, whilst refusing to rest in the stimulation or the sign : never accepting the photograph as a substitute for the living Presence, or mistaking the best and most enchanting of records for the Orphic song.

V

WILL AND LOVE

'THE proper work of the will is to love God.' The relentless drive of our nature towards an undiscerned and yet desired fulfilment can have no other end : and in so far as it has departed from this, its only adequate objective, and frittered its energies on half-real objects of desire, its aim must be corrected by the pressure of Reality.

>Rege quod est devium.

In proportion to our haunting intuition of the Perfect, will be the ceaseless disillusionments which follow our attempt to find and enjoy that Perfect, embodied in the imperfect satisfactions of the temporal world. In so far as we try to rest in them, even the holy incarnations and sacramental actions of religion baffle while they enchant us : for they do not quench but stimulate our metaphysical craving, and point beyond themselves to that all-cherishing, all-penetrating Loveliness which makes them lovely, and can only be known by us in the self-abandonment of love.

>O Lux beatissima,
>Reple cordis intima
>Tuorum fidelium.

136 THE GOLDEN SEQUENCE

Thus to love God, without demand or measure, in and for Himself—' that we may abide in Him, not that any advantage may accrue to us from Him ' says St. Thomas—this is Charity : and Charity is the spiritual life. Only this most gently powerful of all attractions and all pressures can capture and purify the will of man, and subordinate it to the great purpose of God ; for as His Love and Will are One, so the love and will of man must become one. Therefore all other purifications, disciplines and practices have meaning, because they prepare and contribute to the invasion and transformation of the heart by the uncreated Charity of God. ' Thou art the Love wherewith the heart loves Thee.'

For it is only when the secret thrust of our whole being is thus re-ordered by God and set towards God, that peace is established in the house of life. Then, the disorderly energies of emotion and will are rectified and harmonized, and all the various and wide-spreading love which we pour out towards other souls and things is deepened, unselfed and made safe ; because that which is now sought and loved in them is the immanent Divine thought and love. Thus the will transformed in charity everywhere discovers God. It sees behind and within even the most unpleasing creatures the all-pleasing Creator ; and loves and cherishes, in and for Him, that which in itself never could be loved. It discerns and adores His mysterious action within the most homely activities and most disconcerting frustrations of the common life. And by this

WILL AND LOVE

humble and glad recognition of that secret Presence, all the apprehensions of the senses, all the conceivings of the mind, all the hoarded treasures and experiences of the past, are cleansed and sanctified.

Veni, lumen cordium.

Nothing but the power and pressure of the Absolute Love, humbling while it quickens and delights, can do this for us : shedding the light of charity on our conflicts and problems, persuading the restless will to cease its arrogant and restless strivings, and producing that living and supple detachment—using all gifts for God alone, and doing all works within and for His love—which is the secret of freedom and joy. ' The closer a soul approaches God by love ', says Maritain, ' the simpler grows the gaze of her intelligence, and the clearer her vision.' We may be utterly bewildered by the world of faith when it is presented to our understanding, and daunted by the effort which is demanded if we are to lose the life of memory in forward-tending hope. But the simple penetration of the Divine Charity neither bewilders nor daunts us. The soul simplified in charity can go in and out, and find pasture at every level. All things work together, because all has been laid open to the consecrating and clarifying action of the Divine Love ; and all becomes in fact a medium for the recognition and expression of that love.

This transforming of the will in love, this simplifying and supernaturalizing of the whole drive and intention of our life, by its immersion in the great movement of the Infinite Life, is itself the work of Creative Spirit. It is only possible because that Spirit already indwells the soul's ground, and there pursues the secret alchemy of love ; more and more possessing and transmuting us, with every small movement of acceptance or renunciation in which we yield ourselves to the quiet action of God. It is true that the soul hardly perceives the separate moments of this mysterious action ; and only by a view which takes in long stretches of experience, can realize the changes which it works.

Yet our own self-discipline and suffering, our willing acquiescence and adjustment to circumstances, could do little here, did they not work together with the inciting, moulding, indwelling Power ; submitting us to that secret and passive purification which cleanses will and emotion of unreal attachments, and perfectly unites the poor little love and will of man with the universal Love and Will of God. Then, when the whole movement of our being is freely given in love to the purposes of Spirit, and takes its small place in the eternal order, we find our place and our peace. We learn to give significance and worth to our homeliest duties by linking all the chain-like activities of daily life with His overruling and unchanging Reality : ' that most inspiring and darling relation ', says Von Hügel, wherein ' you have each single act, each single moment, joined directly to God—Himself not a

WILL AND LOVE

chain, but one great Simultaneity'. And if we ask why this self-giving to the vast Divine action, rather than an individual self-fulfilment, is the goal of spiritual man ; the answer is that any other makes nonsense of our life, gives it no meaning which is adequate to its cravings and its powers.

> Sine tuo numine,
> Nihil est in homine,
> Nihil est innoxium.

Here, then, reason and love combine to assure us that our end is God alone ; first realized as an influence, one amongst other claims and objects of desire, and then, as we more and more respond to His attraction, as the only satisfaction of the heart ; and at last as the all-penetrating, all-compelling Reality, that only Life which is recognized by faith, desired in hope, achieved by Charity. Then, all those separate movements of love and longing—those passionate self-givings and agonies of desire—in which the struggling and half-awakened spirit reaches out towards life and draws back to the prison of solitary pain, find their solution and satisfaction in God ; and there is established in her that steadfast habitude of love which makes of her the open channel and docile instrument of the one Divine Love. 'Who dwelleth in Charity dwelleth in God, and God in him' : for the secret of Charity is an opening up of the whole tangled, many-levelled creature to the penetration of that Spirit which already indwells our soul's ground.

Then the deep and gentle power of the Unchanging quickens, possesses and directs the changeful self; by its silent pressure perpetually reminding us of the disharmonies and wasteful follies of our claimful and divided life, purifying our inward trend and effort, and turning our nature in its wholeness towards the purposes of God : till at last the steady soul, purified in love and become one will with the hidden all-loving Will, can maintain her easy poise and orientation, her quiet gaze on God, within the wild confusing dance of life.

' Though we here speak of love ', say Barbanson, ' I would rather term it the divine Spirit, lest some should mistakenly adhere more to the effect than to the cause, which is God himself. For love is but an effect and operation of the divine Spirit. I mean not only that more impetuous and violent love which is in the heart and inferior affective part ; but also, and more, that love which resides in the supreme will, sweetly informing and filling it with such a divine motion.'

This cleansing, bracing and transforming of the will and emotional life is the hardest and most searching of all the soul's purifications. For it requires us to take the Cross into the most hidden sanctuary of personality, and complete that living sacrifice which the mortifying of the senses began. Now we must be ready not merely to renounce natural self-fulfilment and consolation, but supernatural self-fulfilment and consolation too ; placing ourselves without reserve in the hand of God, and

WILL AND LOVE

subordinating our small interests to the deep requirements of His mysterious life. As human love only achieves nobility when *Eros* is converted into *Agape*, when crude desire is sublimated, and becomes a self-giving, tenderness ; so with the craving for God which possesses all awakened souls. Only in so far as it compels us to a single undemanding act of self-giving can it be reckoned as purged of self-love ; and only this simple and unconditioned charity can make of the soul a point of insertion for the action of the Spirit within the human world—a tool of the Divine creative will.

This transformation of the will by Charity is chiefly accomplished, and perhaps most deeply and painfully experienced, in the life of prayer. For here the self-regarding instincts of greed, lust and avarice find their last refuge, and ceaselessly invite the devout to a self-regarding spirituality, a seeking of spiritual enjoyment, a hoarding of spiritual wealth. And here the purging influence of the Love of God is chiefly felt in terms of deprivation. It is true that those short and indescribable moments, when the soul seems without sign or image to savour God, are alone completely happy and unstrained. Then she is absorbed and penetrated by a life that is peace. Yet this feeling of beatitude is not Charity. For Charity requires an entire detachment of the will from pleasurable feeling, willingness to embrace a dry and unconsoled prayer, or a vocation that seems to exclude all but the virtual communion of a ceaseless self-abandonment.

What is asked is the unselfing of the whole drive of our God-given nature, its detachment from all softness and ease, all personal enjoyment and achievement, even of the most apparently spiritual kind : and only the hard lessons of dereliction will accomplish this. It is a rough training, designed to make of those who can endure it the hardy and devoted fellow-workers with Spirit ; not the hothouse products of an intensive piety. Charity must not seek her own spiritual comfort, or attribute any importance to her own spiritual apprehensions. As poor yet making many rich, as having nothing yet possessing all things, she must achieve the perfect suppleness, the undivided vigour, of the self-abandoned but energetic will : not the limp acquiescence of the quietist.

The detachment of the soul from the mere enjoyment of its spiritual correspondences, the transformation of the easy-going amateur into the disciplined professional, is mainly achieved in and through our own psychic and emotional instability ; ever betraying us, and making impossible the steady enjoyment of light and of consoling prayer. Here as elsewhere the suffering which enters by the door of our own weakness is always the most humbling and purifying in the end. By these inevitable alternations of our spiritual sensitiveness, our spiritual life is detached from feeling and grounded in faith ; centred in God and not in spiritual self. For strong and ardent souls, this final purging of the will may be a desperate crisis ;

WILL AND LOVE

a darkness and storm in which it seems as though the little boat must founder, a testing to the utmost of fortitude and of trust. 'For suddenly, or ever thou knowest', says the Epistle of Privy Counsel, 'all is away and thou left barren in the boat, blowing with blundering blasts now hither and now thither, thou knowest never where nor whither. Yet be not abashed, for He shall come, I promise thee, full soon when He liketh, to relieve thee and doughtily deliver thee of all thy dole . . . and all this He doth because He will have thee made as pliant to His will ghostly, as a roan glove to thine hand bodily.'

Such a pliability, which accepts without reluctance and in peace the strange movements of the Hand of God, the unexplained vicissitudes of a spiritual course, is a great earnest of Charity. For only a very loving self-oblivion can follow the hard counsel of St. Francis de Sales, and 'refuse to be troubled because we are being troubled, or disquieted because we are unquiet'. Yet those who love much, think little of the weather. Even though the further outlook be unsettled, and the visibility far from good, they are always ready to go forward 'with the wind and rain in their face'. They are convinced that a dark and arduous prayer, void of self-interest, and basing all on the steady direction of the pure bare will to God, unites them more closely to their Pattern than those devotional enjoyments which were so conspicuously absent from His life. From beginning to end Christ never sought for Himself any spiritual advantage or consolation. His steadfast will and perfect love accepted evenly that which was uneven, and went without reluctance from Hermon to Gethsemane. In the agony of the Passion, He sacrificed the dearest treasure of His secret life. All the triumphs of the Spirit have been won through those who here ' follow the footsteps of His holy life ' and are clear of all taint of spiritual avarice, all selfish longing for personal beatitude.

So the final cleansing of the will and heart requires the soul to disregard her own inevitable alternations of pain and pleasure, communion and dereliction ; to escape from introspection and subjectivity into the bracing atmosphere of God. She is to lose herself in the great Divine purpose, and in His will find her unbreakable peace. For though this final transforming action of Spirit on the soul is first experienced as a purifying inward suffering, while our conscious disharmony with God persists ; when the soul has at last become pliant to Him and His interests, it enters into a very quiet and unanalysed condition of freedom and of joy.

Da perenne gaudium.

The saints have ever sought with an increasing ardour this simple and self-oblivious ideal. As faith and hope more utterly possessed them and subdued to one purpose all the powers of the soul, so an entire and loving self-donation in and through circumstance has seemed to them to contain within itself the whole substance of a spiritual life. ' What require I more of thee, than that thou shouldst study wholly to resign thyself to me ? ' Indeed, it is the beggar-maid's only possible response to Cophetua : for all that she has is her will and her love.

PRAYER

I

THE SPAN OF PRAYER

WITHIN the living experience of the soul it is impossible to separate the spheres of purification and of prayer; for this breaks up the solidarity of that Godward life of man, which is at the same time an ever-renewed movement of abandonment, an intercourse, and a transformation. The life of prayer, in its widest and deepest sense, is our total life towards and in God; and therefore the most searching of all the purifying influences at work in us. It is the very expression of our spiritual status, a status at once so abject, and so august; the name of the mysterious intercourse of the created spirit with that Uncreated Spirit, in whom it has its being and on whom it depends. We are called, as the New Testament writers insist, to be ' partakers of the Divine Nature ' : and this is a vocation which shames while it transforms. So prayer may be, and should be, both cleansing and quickening: by turns conversation and adoration, penitence and happiness, work and rest, submission and demand. It should have all the freedom and variety, the depth and breadth of life; for it is in fact the most fundamental expression of our life. And though it is and must be developed by means of a deliberate discipline, and through the humble practice of symbolic acts, these only have importance because they set free the will from unreal objectives, and help our whole being to expand towards God.

In all its degrees, from the most naïve to the most transcendental, and in all its expressions—from the most simple and homely devotional acts, to that passive waiting on the Spirit, 'idle in appearance, and yet so active', which is called by Grou 'the adoration most worthy of God'—the very heart of prayer is this opening up of human personality to the all-penetrating and all-purifying Divine activity. On one hand, we acknowledge our need and our dependence; on the other the certain presence of the supernatural world, the *Patria* ever in intimate contact with us, and our own possession of a seed, a supernatural spark, which knows that world and corresponds with it. Thus all progress in prayer, whatever its apparent form or achievements, consists in the development of this, its essential character. It must nourish and deepen our humility, confidence and love; and thus set up and maintain an ever more perfect commerce between the soul's true being and that Being in Whom it lives and moves. This is why, in the concrete reality of the interior life, prayer and purification must always go hand in hand.

THE SPAN OF PRAYER

For this mysterious intercourse, so crudely and so casually practised by us, so little understood, places our souls—conditioned as they are by succession and contingency—at the disposal of that immanent Spirit of God which indwells and penetrates our life, and yet transcends succession and contingency. It is a movement out towards absolute action ; man the ever-changing acknowledging the presence and reality of the Changeless, and adhering to It in trustful love. This communion with the Supernatural then, whether active or passive, interceding or adoring—for all these are the partial expressions of one rich and various correspondence—is the religious act, the religious state *par excellence* ; the very substance of a spiritual life. The apparatus of institutional religion, its verbal and visual suggestions, its symbolic acts, are intended to evoke, nourish, organize and direct it. The form it will take in any one life, will depend on that soul's particular situation and type ; the prayer itself, whether active or passive, corporate or secret, will always consist in a profound and active correspondence with the Spirit, more and more recognized as the inspiring cause of all we do and are. Devotional words and deeds, meditation, aspiration, recollection and the rest, are there to help us to evoke and maintain this, which alone matters ; to steady the vagrant imagination, give us suitable suggestions, teach and tranquillize our souls. In meditation, says Surin, we go to God on foot ; in the prayer of affection we go on horseback ;

in the prayer of simple recollection we sail in a good ship with a favouring wind. The essential thing is that we should undertake the journey; that the soul's face should be set towards its home.

Yet, because prayer is indeed a supernatural act, a movement of spirit towards Spirit, it is an act which the natural creature can never begin or complete in his own power. Though it seems to him to be by his own free choice and movement that he lifts up his soul towards God, it is in truth this all-penetrating God, who by His secret humble pressure stirs man to make this first movement of will and love. The apparent spontaneity, the exercise of our limited freedom—genuinely ours, and most necessary to the soul's health—are yet entirely dependent on this prevenient and overruling Presence, acting with power and gentleness in the soul's ground. Progress in prayer is perhaps most safely measured by our increasing recognition of this action, the extent in which Spirit ' prays in us ' and we co-operate with it : till, in the apparently passive and yet most powerful prayer of the great contemplative, the consciousness of our own busy activity is entirely lost in the movement of the Divine will, and the soul is well content to ' let Another act in her '.

But having said this, we must at once add that here, as elsewhere in the spiritual life, the action of God is always felt to deepen, stimulate and direct the self's own action—never to abolish it. The ' holy passivity ' of the extreme quietist is

THE SPAN OF PRAYER 151

coma, not contemplation. Again and again experience endorses the axiom of St. Thomas : ' God's grace and man's will rise and fall together.' And if by ' grace ' we mean, as we should, the actual self-giving of the immanent Divine Life, the personal, manward-tending, love and will of God ; then prayer, from the human side, begins with man's response to God's incitement. It is the movement and expression, part-effort, part-surrender, of his Godward-tending love and will. ' A certain impulse of the will tending to God with all its strength ', says Malaval, is the first point of real prayer.

This means that even the most passive prayer shall never be a state of limp dependence. Concealed within its quiet is a vigorous and yet humble co-operation with Spirit's ceaseless action ; sanctifying and sensitizing our spirits, and turning them to the purposes of Eternal Life. Though all that really matters is indeed done to us and not by us, and we realize this more and more fully as the life of prayer proceeds and deepens our creaturely sense, the ' marvellous intercourse between finite and Infinite ' is a genuine communion. It demands the deliberate use of our initiative and will. Acknowledging that we can do little, we must yet do all that we can : be alert to look, listen and adhere. The asking, seeking, knocking of the Gospel, are surely the successive stages of an action which at last takes all that we have of determination and desire ; a deliberate ' drawing nigh ' to that only Reality, the Father and living Ocean of all life—

ever ready to pour in on the creature who desires Him, and proves its desire by an exertion of the will, an opening of the soul's door. This is why the great masters of the spiritual life attach so much importance to the form of mental prayer which is known as 'forced acts of the will'; a spiritual and psychological discipline which is often laborious and fatiguing, but unequalled in its power of bringing the reluctant will into ever closer conformity with the Will of God. For real prayer is a mutual act. It is that correspondence between our dependent spirits and His Absolute Spirit, worked partly by grace, but also partly by our wills, which is our mysterious privilege as living children of the Spirit of all spirits, God. This deep communion, this 'prayer which is ceaseless', continues without interruption in the ground of the loving soul.

It is true that in the advanced degrees of prayer, the action of the will is chiefly realized as a total movement of surrender, a mere placing of the soul in God's hand; and the further deep action which follows this surrender is always felt to be the action of God, rather than that of the soul. Hence the exaggerated language of some contemplatives about 'ceasing to act'. But this language really describes their own overwhelming sense of the Divine activity; as the salmon going down-stream might feel itself wholly passive in the powerful current that sweeps it to the sea. Yet the salmon must do some steering, if it is to make the voyage

THE SPAN OF PRAYER

in good order; and maintains itself in the torrent by a thousand subtle movements of adjustment and response. So too that willed surrender, that faithful adherence, which maintains the contemplative in prayer, is itself an action which makes great demands upon the soul—an active and passive co-operation, minute by minute, with the subtle pressures and incitements of God. The Indian teachers of Bhakti devotion describe two ways in which the finite spirit may be abandoned to the Infinite Life: the 'Way of the Cat' and the 'Way of the Monkey'. In the first, the soul is like a helpless kitten in the mother-cat's mouth, carried to safety without any effort on its own part. In the second, it cleaves to God with all its might, like the baby monkey clinging to its mother's breast. The full creative energy of prayer is found in those who follow the monkey-way.

As we are nearest facts when we think of Spirit in terms of Creative Will, so too prayer in its wholeness is best understood in terms of will and intention. Therefore the special form and kind of prayer developed by any one soul matters very little; and distinctions based on the use of set words, the practice of meditation, the degree of abstraction from images, have little more importance than distinctions of custom and dress. All that is required of any 'degree' of prayer is that it should be the unstrained response of the praying soul to its true light and vocation; and so bring it into ever more complete harmony with the immanent Divine will.

And since the vocation of each soul within that great symphony differs, and all are needed for the complete expression of the thought of God, we need not be surprised by the wide diversities, or even the apparent contradictions in *attrait* and in practice, which are found in the world of prayer. We are not to criticize our neighbour's monotonous performance on the triangle, censure the first violin's deliberate silence, or look dubiously at the little bit of score we have received. All contribute to one only music; and this alone gives meaning to their prayer. 'This it is that I ask and desire', says Thomas à Kempis, 'that I may always laud and praise thee.' Some will do this above all in the upward glance of an adoring worship, some by a more intimate love, some by the small offerings of a devoted industry.

Yet something of all these responses of spirit to Spirit must enter and mingle in the full Godward life of every awakened soul; as the hymn of the *Sanctus*, the act of Communion, and the prayer of oblation, have each their necessary part in a perfect Eucharist. For the first gives us realism and awe, protects us from pettiness: it maintains and nourishes the transcendental sense. 'Cease the beholding of yourself and set yourself at nought, and look on Me and see that I am God.' The second warms and strengthens that close personal adherence which is the heart of a spiritual life; enriches awe with deep tenderness, and makes the praying self more and more supple to the delicate

THE SPAN OF PRAYER

pressures of the indwelling Power. The third redeems our prayer from selfishness, and gives to it its special place and function within the mystical body which is built of praying souls. And each of these responses will have its active and its passive form; and often the two will alternate within the self's experience. For passive prayer does not consist in abnormal states of soul, or peculiar feelings. It is simply that deep movement of surrendered love, that muted music, in which our own small action is more and more subordinated to the living Charity of God.

If we turn from this great vision to our own poor practice, and ask what that is or should be, we find that the span of man's actual prayer, his total Godward aspiration, stretches from the extreme of a crude and child-like demand, to the extreme of a disinterested and undemanding adoration, offered to 'God Himself and none of His works'. At one end, we acknowledge our utter and detailed need and dependence on Spirit—our creaturely status—and turn with an instinctive confidence to the hidden richness which can meet that need in all its forms. At the other end, the soul's innate passion for Reality flames out, in awed and delighted worship of the holy loveliness of God. And between these terms, one so homely, and one so august, there is no point at which the intercourse of spirit with Spirit cannot take place.

It is easy for a hurried or fastidious fervour to point out the clear superiority of that worship which 'means only God', and discredit all petitionary prayer. Certainly this is the most primitive and instinctive of all the movements of the soul, and the one that may most easily be tainted by selfishness. Yet a loving and confident relation with our Home and Father, an entire trust in the intimate loving-kindness of the Unseen, a deliberate laying hold on the forces of the spiritual universe, is declared by Christ to be the first point of efficacious prayer. And being small and limited in resources and understanding, we must manage this the best way that we can. 'Ask and ye shall receive . . . every one that asketh receiveth. . . .' Not perhaps the expected answer to its petition; but a disclosure and gift of Spirit, penetrating and transforming our situation, with all its needs and desires. Therefore what matters here is not the thing demanded, the poor range of our asking, but the trustful, childlike temper of the soul; its straightforward relation to God. Where this relation is set up, a new factor enters human experience. Man is in personal and filial touch with that Transcendent Life which penetrates and engulfs him; and because of his acknowledged dependence and confident expectation, he becomes capable of its gifts. For the indwelling Spirit, in His creative freedom, must reach down to, and touch, every need and relationship of His creation. Indeed, He is already present within those relationships—those we call little and those we call great—in the ceaseless activity of His flexible love. Thus the soul deliberately bringing in the

THE SPAN OF PRAYER 157

Divine factor, appealing to it with a realistic trust, does effect a genuine change in every situation so treated ; even though the change may not be apparent on the visible surface of life. So petition or 'impetration' is the naïve expression of a real relationship : all that Origen meant, when he said that 'the Christian life is a prayer'.

It is true that the actual prayer of demand, like all man's religious activities, is a symbolic and dramatic act. We cannot escape this judgement, when we consider the relation of that battering on the doors of heaven, that desperate wrestling with the Spirit to which we are sometimes drawn, with the God Who is ' present everywhere and at all times ' and works in tranquillity within the soul. Yet this urgent and trustful petition, crude though its expression may sometimes be, is the beginning of realistic and efficacious prayer ; and one of the most significant of all the movements of man's spirit. The open beak and expectant trust of the baby bird are a tribute to the mother's faithfulness and love ; an acknowledgement of fact. So, in this ever-renewed movement of supplication, this waiting on God, we express that deep sense of the infinite Generosity on which we depend and our own poverty and need over against it, which is the very heart of man's religion : tempering the awe-struck worship of the Holy by a confident appeal to the Father and Shepherd of souls. As the child said when she first heard the *Te Deum*, ' the splendid bit is where you change the gear '.

II

ADORATION

SURELY the 'marvellous intercourse' of spirit with Spirit which is the essence of a life of prayer, can only begin and be maintained in adoration. The first real response of the awakened creature to the overshadowing and awakening Power, must be a lifting up of mind and heart to God in Himself; the humble, undemanding love of adorer for Adored. Indeed, this awe-struck love must penetrate and sanctify all prayer. Everything is safe which can live within its aura : all is suspect which slurs the deep sense of God's priority and absolute demand. 'Let my prayer be set forth in Thy sight as the incense', says the Psalmist, watching the quiet smoke of that unearthly offering. Its very heart shall be a costly act of purest worship; ascending from visible to Invisible, from changeful man to the Abiding God. It shall not be self-regarding, anxious, utilitarian. It shall be fragrant with adoring love. Then, perhaps, the lifting up of my restless hands towards the Eternal may become as the evening sacrifice ; that meal-offering which hallowed and dedicated the homely stuff of everyday life.

ADORATION

Unless this inarticulate spirit of adoration, the primitive fundamental response of our spirits to God's Spirit, however imperfectly conceived, colours our whole intercourse with Him, we shall not get our proportions right. Without that humble upward look and upward aspiration of the little creature to the Infinite, the life of prayer quickly becomes shallow, cramped, utilitarian ; or even cheaply familiar. For the true situation of the soul entering prayer, is that of the young Isaiah when the glory of the Lord filled the Temple, and he found himself in the presence of a Reality at which even the seraphs dared not look. To forget this, and with it the lessons of the incense and the box of precious ointment, is to cut off our prayer from that which is the very source of its deepest inspiration and power ; the awed yet loving sense of God's absolute primacy, the drawing nigh to Him because He alone matters, and His creatures only matter because of Him.

' If ', says Huvelin, ' a soul said to me, " To-day I saw God," I should ask " How do you feel in yourself, now that God is so near to you, has entered into you ? " If she were indeed penetrated by Him whom she had received she would reply " I find myself very small—I have fallen very low." Confusion of face is the inevitable reaction, the essential impression, of the soul who has seen God pass by in His greatness.' That note of wonder and abasement, the deep feeling of the utter difference in kind between the Eternal God and that creation which He is making for Himself—and yet the marvellous fact, that He desires and incites each created spirit to draw near to Him, and seeks with a greater thirst than He is ever sought: this is never absent from the deepest and most prevailing prayers of the saints.

In Isaiah's vision, those spirits of pure love who stood nearest to the Glory asked for nothing. In deepest reverence, they delighted in God; content to see nothing and do nothing, so long as they were maintained before His face. 'Each one had six wings; with twain he covered his face, and with twain he covered his feet, and with twain he did fly. And one cried unto another, and said, Holy, holy, holy, is the Lord of hosts: the whole earth is full of his glory.' We, drawing near, must at least make an effort to share this point of view. For only that disinterested temper which is lost in the great tide of worshipping love can save our small prayer from sentimentality, self-occupation, the vices of the devotee; and defeat the ignoble tendency to make God useful to man, instead of man useful to God.

So the awe-struck yet confident drawing nigh of the praying soul to the mystery over against it, the lifting up of the eyes of the little creature to that Holy Reality in humble worship—not because it wants something, but because it feels His compelling attraction, the strange magnetism of the Divine—this dim and yet delighted wonder must be the soul's first instinctive response to God's self-revelation. It is a response which seems to arise spontaneously in the very deeps of the natural life, and bind

ADORATION

all creation, conscious and unconscious, into one single act of worship ; praising and magnifying that Absolute Beauty and Truth for and by whom all things are made. There is a story by Osbert Sitwell, which tells how a traveller in the equatorial forests, hearing strange sounds at night, looked out from his window ; and saw in the courtyard, where it was imprisoned, a great anthropoid ape—one of those tragic creatures just verging on the human—bowing in solemn adoration before the splendour of the rising moon. The traveller gazed at this spectacle with awe. ' I had seen ', he said, ' the birth of religion.' Innocent nature emerging from its sleep, and already finding in that first vague moment of consciousness something beyond itself which it must adore ; the first and simplest of the self-disclosures of God, pouring out His strange beauty upon the natural scene, and inviting His creatures' recognition along the channels of sense.

And surely in this primitive, instinctive act of worship, this profound abasement of the creature before the unspeakable mystery over against it, we see something both sacred and fundamental in the relation of all life to God ; the first glimmering consciousness of Supernature, everywhere present, and speaking to the supernatural spark that is buried within us, in a tongue that it can understand. As the Magi came a long and difficult journey, to find that the shepherds were before them ; and even the hurrying shepherds found the animals already in place—so it is deep within the natural order that the embryonic power of prayer, which is at bottom a state or condition of soul rather than a distinct activity, stirs from its sleep.

> Adoro te devote, latens Deitas,
> Quae sub his figuris vere latitas.

Here adoration begins, in a realistic acknowledgement of the Transcendent, however imperfectly understood. For all prayer is first evoked by the gentle self-revelation of Spirit to spirit ; the disclosure of His glory in a way that our limited minds can bear, ' coming down like the rain into a fleece of wool, even as the drops that water the earth '. In the splendour of tropical moonlight ; in those symbolic acts of the religious cult which lead us beyond themselves to Him ; in the persistent and secret touches of Spirit in the soul's deeps, or in the powerful and heart-searching love of some inconspicuous saint, the only Perfect perpetually invites our recognition : and here, to recognize is to adore.

Thus adoration is the first and greatest of life's responses to its spiritual environment ; the first and most fundamental of spirit's movements towards Spirit, the seed from which all other prayer must spring. It is among the most powerful of the educative forces which purify the understanding, form and develop the spiritual life. As we can never know the secret of great art or music until we have learned to look and listen with a self-oblivious reverence, acknowledging a beauty that is beyond our grasp —so the claim and loveliness of God remain un-

ADORATION

realized, till we have learned to look, to listen, to adore. Then only do we go beyond ourselves and our small vision, pour ourselves out to that which we know not, and so escape from our own pettiness and limitations into the universal life.

> Tibi se cor meum totum subjicit
> Quia te contemplans totum deficit.

Adoration can never long remain a private ecstasy. As sometimes in the vast and solemn life of the mountains or the forest, or in the small perfection of a very humble plant, we are suddenly aware of the breathless worship which creation offers to its God; so now we enter into a new relation with that whole created order, and realize our own part in its response to the Creative Love. 'We scale', says Nicholas of Cusa, 'that wall of invisible vision beyond which Infinity is to be found'; join with those who see more than ourselves, and accept the fellowship of those who see less. Our small voices, so feeble in their solitude, augment the one universal chorus of creation; with angels and archangels and all the company of heaven lauding and magnifying one Holy Name.

It is true, that when we come to the practice of this surrendered adoration, so difficult to the troubled and arrogant soul of the modern world, we discover with a certain astonishment that there is much less difference than we like to suppose between our methods and possibilities and those of the primitive; already stirred by a spirit that he knows not to abase himself before the mystery of the Unseen. We bring, as St. Paul would say, our 'carnal' inheritance with us, and share his childlike status over against the Reality of God. Thus we worship, not yet in spirit or in truth, but as best we can. As the primitive sought to express his deep emotion in ritual action, his naïve and puzzled sense of the Unseen in myth, we are compelled by our limitations to the same devices. We are still drawn to rhythms and gestures which come to us from the childhood of man; still find significance in practices, of which the lowly origin is hardly concealed. Whether it be the survival or deliberate reproduction of ancient cultus—the Easter taper of tradition, or the votive electric light of the modern shrine—there is surely a deep pathos in these childlike motions of the soul. Again and again men perceive their inadequacy, and again and again revert to this, the natural language of symbol and myth. Thus, ascending to the 'fine point of the spirit' we are yet treading primæval strata all the way; and this is far better, safer and more humbling than trying to make the journey through the air. The world's altar-stairs begin in the jungle; and there is a disconcerting continuity between the first awed and upward look of pithecanthropus and the dark contemplation of the saint. We cannot go far in the life of devotion without being reminded of this humbling solidarity of the race. For man, whether 'civilized' or 'uncivilized', knows very little about the Being of God. The great mountain ranges of

ADORATION 165

His unsearchable majesty are hidden in the clouds ; and the more fully the soul enters the life of prayer, the more deeply it realizes this. Clouds and darkness are round about Him. *Adoro te devote latens Deitas* is the last word of the worshipping spirit, as well as the first.

Yet the whole of life in its splendour and contrasts, seen with the eyes of humble admiration, will give us hints and intimations of that Reality and that Presence which transcends and supports it ; and points beyond itself to the Perfection on which it depends. God, who is there before us, invites our delighted praise along a thousand paths. Limited incarnations and disclosures of the Eternal, moulding the web of things to His revealing purpose, and using the rich beauty of creation to convey a Beauty Increate, perpetually stir to life our latent tendency to awe-struck worship. Love and sacrifice in humble places guarantee the Love that moves the stars.

For Christian experience, the life and person of Christ stand apart as the greatest of these self-revelations ; the perfect self-expression of the Holy in human terms, and the supreme school and focus of man's adoring prayer. For here the Invisible God, by the most wonderful of His condescensions, discloses His beauty and attraction—the brightness of His glory and the express image of His person—in a way that is mercifully adapted to our limitations, and meets us on our own ground. Therefore the events of Christ's life—alike the most strange and the most homely—are truly 'mysteries'. They contain far more than they reveal. They are charged with Spirit, and convey the supernatural to those who are content to watch and adore. Because of this, Christian devotion moves ever to and fro between adoring and intimate prayer; passing through the incarnational veil to the Absolute Beauty, and returning to find the Absolute Beauty shining through the incarnational veil. 'Let thy thoughts be always upward to God and direct thy prayer to Christ continually,' says Thomas à Kempis. Thus the great horizon gives its meaning to the welcoming figure; and the welcoming figure makes the great horizon safe and fair.

And here the soul's actual prayer will be a reflection of its whole life. The only preparation for such an adoring approach to Spirit, is a daily response to circumstance which is coloured by the delighted reverence that finds the natural scene and all its contacts and relationships, its sufferings and enjoyments, sacred for the sake of His indwelling and overshadowing Life. 'The Holy Spirit', says Grou, 'will either govern all your actions, or cease to govern your prayer.' It is only when life and prayer are thus well mixed together, that the atmosphere has been created in which the work of prayer can be done. For it is within this penetrating and awestruck sense of God Present, not as one among other facts and demands, but as the one real Fact and Demand ever pressing on His creature, that self-giving to His purposes emerges and grows. Adoration, for the soul which has truly learnt it, will, as it more and more possesses the praying spirit, lead on to self-offering. Then the deep prayer in which we pass away from our preoccupations and sink down into the soul's ground, will tend more and more to become a very simple act of self-abandoned love. And as each great phase of the life of prayer ever tends to pass over into silence, so this. First the best words and rhythms that men have found, to stir and maintain the mind and heart in its worship of Reality : and then the pause and hush of a delighted homage : and at last something so absolute, that the creature is lost in an act of praise which possesses, engulfs, transcends its very life.

III

COMMUNION

THE prayer of adoration must end on the cry of St. Augustine : ' Lord, I seek not to penetrate thy lofty nature, for in no way do I compare my understanding with it.' For the more deeply we enter the worshipping life, the more profoundly we experience the transcendence and the otherness of That which we adore : and the more deeply purifying is the failure of our understanding before the reality of God. And were this meek, objective worship the beginning and end of our relation with Reality, the note of ceaseless joy on which the Golden Sequence closes could never be heard in human prayer. But all is not over, because the Radiance that attracts also daunts us, and one side of our response to Spirit must always be a humble acknowledgement of our ignorance and nothingness before the rich simplicity of God. For that rich simplicity has a certain kinship with the creature, which It is ever moulding and creating both from without and from within. Spirit indwells and penetrates the soul's very fabric as a quiet Love ; and it is here, in our ground, that we are to experience the most intimate and transforming

COMMUNION

realities of Prayer. Here we may come to know by the penetration of the heart, that which we can never understand by the exercise of the mind.

For the life of prayer, in its full and balanced development, unites a width and depth of vision with a great interior dependence and intimacy. The vision of God and the love of God complete each other; one expands and enlightens, the other humbles, deepens and enslaves the soul. So long as we are human, both thought and feeling must enter into our response to surrounding realities; and in the life of prayer this thought and feeling, touched by the Supernatural, become transformed into a great awe and a great love. Thus the prayer of adoration passes almost insensibly into the prayer of communion and self-offering, as worship becomes more realistic, more deeply coloured by love. Indeed it has sometimes been said that adoration and self-giving together cover the whole ground of human prayer.

But this description is only adequate to prayer as seen from our side, and expressed within our poor categories. In its wholeness, it is something at once more subtle, more rich and free than this. It is a give-and-take, a conversation, between Spirit and spirit. 'May thy treasures be laid open to me', said St. Ethelwold, 'and my mind laid open to thee.' We only give, or want to give, because He gives first; are only driven towards Him because, as the old mystic says, He already 'has his sail in our ship'.

THE GOLDEN SEQUENCE

> Veni, pater pauperum,
> Veni, dator munerum,
> Veni, lumen cordium.

Of this generous coming of the Spirit is born all human prayer. Hence that which is adoration when it turns toward God Infinite, deepens to the sacred wonder of communion, when it turns towards God Intimate.

> Dulcis hospes animae !

This too represents or suggests under human symbols a most real and clear experience, a real relationship between the eternal Father of Spirits and the childlike praying soul : a loving intercourse with That which is far beyond us, and yet is found to be divinely near.

And here it is that penitence enters most fully into prayer. For when we thus recognize the gentle touch of the Holy and the Perfect on our smudged imperfect selves ; then contrition, because our response is so impaired by slackness, self-indulgence and sin, overwhelms and humbles us. And in so doing it opens our souls to the purifying action of Spirit, softens and tranquillizes, and increases our capacity for God. ' How delicately thou teachest love to me ! ' says St. John of the Cross. If we are ever to learn it, we must be ready to move with suppleness between the most unearthly and most personal recognitions. We must recognize our own poverty over against the generous Divine richness ; our own guilt in respect of the crucifixion of Divine

Love. We must by turns ascend to the spire-top of the spirit, and sink into the deeps of the soul's ground. For all the resources of poetry, and all the contrasting images and experiences of man's emotional life, can only suggest but never give the content of this simple yet incredible intercourse between the fugitive in its weakness and instability, and the Abiding in its infinite power.

In this developed prayer of communion, however simple and inarticulate its form may be, a strange sympathy is set up between the soul and its Home and Father. Dimly yet quite truly, we begin to be conscious of a steady supple pressure, felt both within and without the soul; and a loving peaceful joy in the great purposes of Spirit, swamping all personal anxiety and desire. 'For God', says Malaval, 'who has created the soul, and is himself pure Spirit, knows better than any one else can know how to speak to the spirit: which is, in reality, to act upon it, not with tumult, trouble or agitation but in solid peace and profound tranquillity.' And because of this sympathy, this deep and tender communion which is the consummation of self-giving, we find we possess a certain dark but real understanding of the Will, Desire, Direction, of the Mind of God; we have a sure sense of being taught and disciplined through all the events that come to us, and through His touches felt in our very substance; overshadowed and guided in choices and moments of crisis, in giving guidance to others, in distinguishing the real and false issues of life. And although we must still ' direct our wills vigorously towards God ', maintaining our adherence with steadiness and courage, as the baby monkey clings with all its might ; still, more and more all that matters seems to be given us, we share more and more fully the generous and life-giving Life.

> In labore requies,
> In aestu temperies,
> In fletu solatium.

Perhaps the simple contemplation to which many souls are drawn, is best understood as a dim realization of this status. For if, outside prayer, the soul interrogates her own experience, and asks what it is that so firmly stops or else so quietly absorbs her own activity, it is surely the sense of all being done by Another, to whom she adheres—a Presence which has absolute priority within her life. St. Patrick in his ' Confession ' tells how one night he saw in vision Christ praying within his soul ; and he heard a voice which said ' I am that Spirit, which prays in thee and above thee '. So too we know ourselves at last to be gathered into a greater Life, at once personal and infinite, in us and above us, and there feel at home ; as, on natural levels, we feel at home in our ordinary objective world.

Mystics, trying to tell us of their condition, often say that they feel ' sunk in God like a fish in the sea '. We pass over these phrases very easily, and forget that they are the final result of a struggle to find the best image for an admittedly imageless truth.

COMMUNION

Yet prayer is above all the act in which we give ourselves to our soul's true Patria ; enter again that Ocean of God which is at once our origin and our inheritance, and there find ourselves mysteriously at home. And this strange, home-like feeling kills the dread which might overcome us, if we thought of the unmeasured depths beneath us, and the infinite extent and utter mystery of that Ocean into which we have plunged. As it is, a curious blend of confidence and entire abandonment keep us, because of our very littleness, in peace and joy : content with our limited powers and the limitless Love in which we are held. Nothing in all nature is so lovely and so vigorous, so perfectly at home in its environment, as a fish in the sea. Its surroundings give to it a beauty, quality, and power which is not its own. We take it out, and at once a poor, limp dull thing, fit for nothing, is gasping away its life. So the soul sunk in God, living the life of prayer, is supported, filled, transformed in beauty, by a vitality and a power which are not its own. The souls of the saints are so powerful because they are thus utterly immersed in the Spirit : their whole life is a prayer. The Life in which they live and move and have their being gives them something of its own quality. So long as they maintain themselves within it, they are adequate to its demands, because fed by its gifts. This re-entrance into our Origin and acceptance of our true inheritance is the supernatural life of prayer, as it may be experienced by the human soul. Far better to be a shrimp within that ocean, than a full-sized theological whale cast upon the shore.

In our own small practice this deep and simple communion may be given to us under the most personal or impersonal symbols. For some it is centred on Christ's person; and experienced as a still abiding in the aura of the beloved Presence. All the poetry of Christocentric devotion is born of this type of prayer. Sometimes, as in sacramental communion, the soul is aware of a positive inflow of the Divine Charity and Peace. Sometimes the quiet brooding on a word, a phrase, a mystery—a tranquil chewing of the evangelical cud—though it does not seem to give fresh food or knowledge, does give or revive in us the very flavour of God ' having in itself all sweetness and all savour ', and draws us into a communion that is beyond speech. Sometimes the ' rapt spright ' is subdued to an Action which has no image, and of which we can say nothing at all.

Or this prayer may be realized by way of a general and increasing tendency of the soul to recollect itself in God, entering at last a silence of peculiar quality, sometimes dry and costly, sometimes deeply joyful; when we hardly know where we are or what is done to us, or why it is imperative that our own activity should cease. Whatever its form, we need not hope to maintain this state for long periods, at least as a conscious experience. It should be accepted and relinquished, humbly and without strain : for it always appears to the self as something 'given', which cannot be procured by any exercise of the will and only presupposes the readiness of the heart.

Here variety in method and in *attrait* seem to matter very little. In all one Spirit works, adopting and overruling the fragmentary contributions, movements and stimulations of memory, sense and thought. Bérulle, who has spoken most deeply, and yet most simply, of the life of prayer, describes it as a threefold relation of the soul with God; adoring, adhering, and co-operating. Thus adoration is the root, communion the flower, intercessory action the fruit, of that divine-human love which binds in one the total life of prayer. And these three responses of spirit to Spirit, all of which must enter into the full prayer of the awakened creature, are simultaneous not successive: even though they will be present in varying proportions within each life, and at each stage of the soul's growth. For they mean the surrender and satisfaction of mind, of heart, and of will; and each depends for its full and perfect exercise on all. Only the heart and mind purified by the rigours of bare faith, and disciplined to adoration, can accept the wonder of a Reality which meets it within its own frontiers, is already present in every fibre of its being, and asks only for its self-giving love; and only a soul in which that deep communion is established can co-operate with the Divine energy at work within the world of souls and things.

So even this deep and satisfying communion of

spirit with Spirit, which more and more dominates those lives that are becoming sensitive to God, is found to point beyond itself. It may never be accepted and enjoyed as a private satisfaction. It looks towards some creative goal; general or particular, remote or immediate. It has a definite place within the eternal purpose, because it puts the half-grown soul at the disposal of the moulding Spirit in a way that nothing else can do. If we give a sufficiently wide and deep meaning to our terms, this is true even of the most apparently passive and formless prayer of contemplation; which seems to the praying soul to be no more than the expression of its own thirst for self-abandonment, and merely to place it in the Hand of God. For since the aim of the immanent Divine Will is the supernaturalization of all life, and prayer is a sovereign means by which the Divine immanence works on, in, and through the heart and will of man, we cannot deny creative purpose even to such passive and generalized prayer. It is indeed always declared by the mystics to have profound effects, which are not limited by its transforming action on personality. They regard it as the medium of an actual conveyance of life, and hence the direct cause of their powers. 'In this prayer', says Grou, 'stripped of image and apperception . . . the soul *unites herself to God in her ground;* the created intelligence to Uncreated Intelligence, without the intervention of imagination or reasoning or anything else but a very simple attention of the mind and an equally simple application of the will.'

COMMUNION

And by this simple union and this tranquil application of a self-abandoned love, the soul becomes the tool and channel of the Creative Love.

Thus communion and intercession, adherence and collaboration, can never be separated in experience. They are completing aspects of that total life of prayer, of which the key-word is to be *fiat voluntas tua*. Even while it moves, within the action of God, towards that complete surrender which puts it, in action and in contemplation, wholly at the disposal of the Creative Will, this life moves also to a discovery and fulfilment of its own unique task within the mystical body of praying souls.

IV

ACTION

'GOD', says Pascal, 'has established prayer, in order to communicate to His creatures the dignity of causality.' He delegates to our half-grown spirits something of His own power and freedom ; allows our wills, under His incitement, and in union with His own, to originate action upon spiritual levels, exert influence within the web of circumstance. Christ's teaching about prayer emphasizes its energetic power ; and suggests that we by our confident action evoke a responsive movement from the enfolding spiritual world. This is intercession ; that creative prayer which crowns the life of adoration and communion. For the goal of this life can never be a sterile beatitude, a 'divine duet' between God and the soul. It must always point beyond itself. Even the purest prayer of adoring contemplation and self-mergence needs for its justification the whole economy of that spiritual universe within which it arises, to which it contributes, and by which it is fed.

For the aim of soul's self-giving to Spirit, and Spirit's possession of soul, is that the soul may expand, become more deeply living and creative,

ACTION

and be woven into that spiritual body, the Invisible Church, through which the work of the Spirit is done. The great liturgic action of the Church Visible, its ceaseless corporate life of intercession, self-offering, adoration, only has meaning as the outward expression of this mystery of 'the Spirit and the Bride'. And on the other hand, the personal life of prayer only has its meaning, because it is part of that great life-process, of which the limits are unknown to us, and which is bringing in the Kingdom of God. And hence, its full exercise is only possible where the Divine Charity purifies and possesses the soul. As adoration led on and in, to a personal relationship of communion and self-offering ; so, from that entire self-offering—and not otherwise—there develops the full massive and active prayer in which the human spirit becomes in a mysterious way the fellow-worker with the Holy Spirit of Creation ; a channel or instrument through which that Spirit's work is done, and His power flows out to other souls and things. The dynamic Love of God, moving secretly and quietly within the web of circumstance, finds in the man of prayer the most subtle and powerful of its tools.

'Thou hast made us for Thyself' : not only to be worshippers, but to be workmen. The will transformed in charity, and united with that power of God which indwells our finite spirits, can and does reach out by supplication, by immolation, by suffering, or by a steady and a patient love; to rescue, heal, change, give support and light. In and through it is manifested some small ray of the saving and redeeming power of God. That is real intercession ; a spiritual activity which is entirely misunderstood by us, if we think of it merely in terms of petition. For real intercession is in the last resort a part of the creative action of God, exercised through those created spirits which have achieved a certain union with Him. And it requires for its real and safe exercise that temper of humble worship, and that habitude of docile correspondence, which the life of adoration and communion develops in the soul. Only a will that is purified and nourished by the indwelling Spirit and confirmed in the humble knowledge of its own dependent state, can recognize those quiet pressures which indicate the path its intercessions should take, and subordinate its work for souls to the overruling Divine Will : preserved from perverse desires and vagrant choices by its meek and adoring inclination towards God.

For as there is a counterfeit devotion which ministers to spiritual self-interest and self-love, and is content with a greedy enjoyment of the sweetness of prayer ; so there is also a counterfeit intercession, which may be merely the disguised exercise of a vigorous but unsurrendered will—not self-given for the promotion of the Divine purpose, but demanding the fulfilment at all costs of its own desires. This, and this only, is open to the common accusation of ' trying to change the mind of God '. For here the aim is not a self-abandoned collaboration in His unseen purpose, the conveyance of grace or healing

ACTION 181

in accordance with a hidden design ; but the achievement of self-chosen ends, the particular success, conversion, rescue, or recovery on which our determination is set.

It is even possible that such a vigorous action of the will under the form of impetration may achieve its object, and snatch a dubious triumph ; as our wilful intervention on the physical plane may sometimes enjoy an undesirable success. But this effective employment of our psychic energy is not to be claimed as an 'answer to prayer'; and is not necessarily in accordance with the Spirit's will. The mysterious power of mutual influence is little understood. But at least we know that it can operate on many levels, some of them less than spiritual ; and in many directions, not all of which may lie in the direction of the Mind of God. That this should be possible is inherent in our limited freedom, and brings with it the capacity for going wrong, and even perhaps for doing harm. There may therefore be real danger in the persistent exercise of a strong and unmortified will, an obstinate choice, a passionate craving, under the appearances of prayer. It is clear, for instance, that the fervent and competing supplications born of national or sectarian intolerance, which demand with complete assurance the failure or success of military operations, the triumph of opposite doctrinal views, or the conversion of individuals from or to a particular Christian Church, cannot all be the work of the Spirit Who ' prays in us and above us '. Yet these acts of will make their contribution to our invisible environment ; and in proportion to their vigour may produce a certain effect upon the psychic atmosphere.

It is true that in so far as any desire, however crude or mistaken, is really lifted up with confident trust into the spiritual realm, it is thereby cleansed and made safe ; and may, in proportion to the praying soul's docility, be transformed into a channel of grace, unrecognized perhaps as an ' answer ' yet truly the response of Spirit to the Godward movement of the soul's desire. For here there has been an appeal to the Holy ; a virtual acknowledgement of its priority, which involves real subordination to its Will, even though the prayer itself be little better than a yelp of anguish or a desperate appeal for relief. And by this very fact the situation, however little understood by us, is changed ; subdued to the influences of the supernatural world, and brought into immediate contact with the ' power of God to salvation '. This is possible, because intercessory action is always in the last resort the action of the Spirit using the human creature as its tool.

But this means once more that the will transformed in Charity, the desire which has been brought to Gethsemane and subordinated to the purposes of the Spirit—fusing all distinct petitions in the great *Fiat* of surrendered love—is alone fully effective and entirely safe. So the final purification in love of the human spirit, and the full achievement of its peculiar destiny as a collaborator in the Spirit's work, must go together : obverse and reverse of the unitive life.

ACTION

Then the soul's total prayer enters, and is absorbed into, that ceaseless Divine action by which the created order is maintained and transformed. For by the prayer of self-abandonment, she enters another region; and by adherence is established in it. There, the strange energy of will that is in us and so often wasted on unworthy ends, can be applied for the world's needs—sometimes in particular actions, sometimes by absorption into the pure Act of God.

For all real prayer is part of the Divine action. It is, as St. Paul says, Spirit that prays in us; and through and in this prayer exerts a transforming influence upon the created world of souls and things. But the path and method of this deep essential prayer may vary between the saint's entire self-immolation for the world's sin, and that symbolic battering at the doors of heaven, that agony of petition by which many souls actualize their ardent desire. All the apparatus of verbal intercession, with its lists and litanies and intentions, is meant to deepen and give precision to that intercessory life which shall gradually include in its span all the deeds, renunciations and sufferings of the soul; and is itself a small part of that redeeming life, by which Spirit purifies nature and makes it susceptible of God. Thus the object of intercessory action may be general or particular, spiritual or physical. It may concern the most homely or transcendental levels of life: the fulfilment of little hopes or of great ideals. Or it may seek without ceasing that restoration to wholeness of life of the diseased or the sinful, which must always lie within the will of the Creative Love.

For the prayer of a wide-open and surrendered human spirit appears to be a major channel for the free action of that Spirit of God with whom this soul is ' united in her ground '. Thus it seems certain that the energy of prayer can and does avail for the actual modifying of circumstance ; the renewing of physical health ; the refraining from sin ; and that its currents form an important constituent of that invisible web which moulds and conditions human life. It may open a channel along which power, healing or enlightenment go to those who need them ; as the watering-can provides the channel along which water goes to the thirsty plant. Or the object achieved may be, as we say, ' directly spiritual ' ; the gradual purifying and strengthening, and final sublimation of the praying soul, or of some other particular soul. In all such cases, though much remains mysterious, the connexion between prayer and result does appear as the connexion of genuine cause and effect. Living as we do on the fringe of the great world of Spirit, we lay hold on its mysterious energies and use them in our prayer. We are plainly in the presence of that which Elisabeth Leseur called ' a high and fruitful form of action, the more secure that it is secret ', and only limited by the power and purity of our faith and love.

There is, on the other hand, an intercessory prayer which seems to have no specified aim. It is poured

ACTION 185

out, an offering of love, in order that it may be used ; and this is specially true of its more developed forms in the interior life of devoted souls. As spiritual writers say, its energies and sufferings may simply be 'given to God', added to the total sacrificial action of the Church. It may then do a work which remains for ever unknown to the praying soul ; contributing to the good of the whole universe of spirits, the conquest of evil, the promotion of the Kingdom, the increased energy of holiness. Such general and sacrificial prayer has always formed part of the interior life of the saints ; and is an enduring strand in the corporate work of the Church. It may be done by way of a secret immolation of the heart, by a routine of ordered petitions, or by the solemn ritual of vicarious suffering. It may capture and consecrate all the homely activities of daily life, and endue them with sacramental power. When St. Teresa founded the discalced Carmelites, it was not to promote the culture of individual souls ; but in order that the corporate hidden prayer and sacrifice of these communities might generate power, combating in some degree the wickedness she saw in the world. It was of this aspect of prayer that Cardinal Mercier spoke, when he said in one of his pastorals, ' Through an ever closer adherence to the Holy Spirit in the sanctuary of your soul, you can, from within your home circle, the heart of your country, the boundary of your parish, overpass all earthly frontiers and . . . intensify and extend the Kingdom of Love.' As the rhythm of Christ's life went to and fro between adoring prayer upon the mountain and the manifestation of the Divine redeeming power in the world, so these two movements should form the rhythm of the life of prayer. For only such a double life can express our double relation to Spirit ; the entire dependence on that which is higher than our highest, and the faithful mediation of that which is nearer than our most inward part.

It is true that many phrases of the great masters of prayer, taken alone and out of their context, seem entirely to exclude this spiritual action of one soul on other souls, for and in God ; and make the life of prayer consist entirely in adoration and adherence. But this contradiction is only apparent : and is simply a vigorous statement of the obligation to put first things first. The adoring surrender of the soul to God, and even a certain union with the immanent Holy Spirit, forms the one essential foundation of all intercessory action. For this action depends primarily, not on the intensity of our sympathetic interest, our psychic sensitiveness, the sustained energy and confidence of our demands, or our telepathic power—though all these may contribute to its effectiveness—but on a profound and selfless devotion to the purposes of the Divine Charity. Even in the crudest, most naïve act of prayer, the soul lays itself open in some degree to that overruling Divine action ; and this movement, initiated by God, is completed and used by Him. Thus the action of God and the soul collaborate in different ways and degrees in every prayer. 'Feelings', 'experiences' and all the rest, fade into insignificance before this most solemn privilege of men.

Here we are surely face to face with one of the great mysteries of that spiritual world in which our real lives are lived; one of the ways in which, as Newman said, we can already 'share the life of saints and angels'—those ordained distributors of the love and power of God. We cannot understand it, but perhaps we grasp its reality better if we keep in mind two facts. The first is, that all experience proves that we are not separate, ring-fenced spirits. We penetrate each other, influence each other for good and evil, for the giving or taking of vitality, all the time. 'Souls, all souls', said Von Hügel, 'are deeply interconnected. The Church at its best and deepest is just that—that interdependence of all the broken and meek, all the self-oblivion, all the reaching out to God and souls. . . . Nothing is more real than this interconnection. We can suffer for one another. No soul is saved alone or by its own efforts.' This accessibility, and this changefulness, is at once our weakness and our strength. And this interaction of souls, this mysterious but most actual communion, depends for its life and reality on God, Spirit, the immanent creative life, Who penetrates and indwells us all, working in and with us. We are all linked in Him. Therefore it is literally true that the secret pressure of the Eternal is present in all movements of mutual service and love.

And the second fact is, that the value and reality

of our souls is at least as much social as individual. We do, and must, reinforce each other ; make good each other's weakness. Each saint has something to give which adds to the glow of all saints : and only by self-loss in that one radiance can make his own life complete. We are woven together, the bright threads and the dull, to form a living tissue susceptible of God, informed by His infinite, self-spending love. ' We have soon ', says Von Hügel again, ' reached the limit of what we ourselves can ever become : it is in joy for the others, for the countless constellations of the spiritual heavens, it is only there—but even there, at bottom, because of God, the Sustainer and fulfiller of all that splendour —that our poor hearts and wills find their peace.'

Thus, intercession is the activity of a spirit which is a member of this living society, this fabric of praying souls penetrated and irradiated by God-Spirit. For this membership gives to each unit a special quality, vigour, power ; a power only given in order that it may be used and shared. Its essence is not the activity of the little soul over against Spirit, but the action of Spirit through and in the little soul self-given to the Spirit's Will. Here we reach the real dignity of the creature, and the very object of the life of prayer : it is able to convey God because it has become susceptible of God. We see this again and again in the lives of the Saints. In the arrogant Sienese scholar, asking the girl Catherine with an insulting pretence of reverence for her prayers, and brought in two days by their steady pressure

ACTION

to an abject and heart-broken penitence. In the Curé d'Ars, drawing to himself and then vanquishing the malice of invisible powers. In the transforming action of Christian philanthropists, whose lives are given to the Spirit's will.

Hence all effective intercession depends on the one hand on the keeping alive of the soul's susceptibility to God, its religious sensitiveness, by constant self-openings towards Him and movements of humble and adoring love ; and on the other hand, on keeping keenly alert to the needs of the world, through an untiring and informed pity and sympathy, ' a wide spreading love to all in common '. Only a charity poured out in both directions can become and remain a channel of the Spirit's Will. And such a vocation in its fullness means much suffering ; a bearing of griefs and a carrying of sorrows, an agonized awareness of sadness and sin. For the great intercessor must possess an extreme sensitiveness to the state and needs of souls and of the world. As those who live very close to nature become tuned to her rhythm, and can discern in solitary moments all the movements of her secret life, or as musicians distinguish each separate note in a great symphony and yet receive the music as one whole ; so the intercessor, whether living in the world or enclosed in a convent (for these are only differences in technique) is sensitized to every note and cadence in the rich and intricate music of the common life. He stretches out over an ever wider area the filaments of love, and receives and endures in his own person the anguish of its sorrow, its helplessness, its confusions, and its sin ; suffering again and again the darkness of Gethsemane and the Cross, as the price of his redemptive power. For it is his awful privilege to stand in the gap between the world's infinite need and the treasuries of the Divine Love.

V

CONCLUSION

AND thus we come back to a humble and homely realism. For we are brought to the recognition that there is indeed a finite created order, truly existing, of which we form part and with which we are designed to correspond. Toward this our human responsibility is absolute. We cannot escape its influence; and may not ignore the appeal of its imperfection to our interest, our pity, and our love. Yet none the less we are in ceaseless contact with an Increate Order, standing over against us in its solemn stillness, and by its energetic Charity penetrating and sustaining our life. With this too we have deep correspondences. It moulds and stimulates us, and seeks to transform us. It is at once the inciting cause and final satisfaction of our metaphysical thirst. The ceaseless creative action of that Spirit on spirit, reaching and shaping us in and through circumstance, and turning our very limitations to the purposes of love—this is the efficient cause of our long purification. The mysterious intercourse between Creator and created is the origin and substance of our prayer.

Thus all that we do and are, whether lofty or

homely, has a double significance and a double reference. It is real in its own right, within the scheme of nature : for the Father and Lover of our souls is the Father and Lover of all life. And beyond this, it mediates the august reality of Supernature ; in so far as we endure in and through it the ceaseless transforming action of God-Spirit. For all our life is sacramental. There is no test, no conflict, no attraction or delight, nor any vicissitude of circumstance which does not come to us charged with Spirit ; no point in the chain of succession where the Eternal cannot be found, served and adored. And in this double status and the double demand which it makes on us, abides the tension and the richness of our mysterious life.

For we are changeful, yet children of the Unchanging ; free and yet dependent ; carnal, sold under sin, and yet perpetually drawn to love and depend on God. We are asked for an utter self-abandonment ; and, in proportion to that self-abandonment, become ever the more vigorous and creative. The true life of the spirit begins with the full and glad acceptance of this situation ; the deletion of the possessive case. ' Send out *thy* light, and *thy* truth ', says the Psalmist : ' all my fountains are in thee ! ' When we know this, we are at peace.

> Veni, Sancte Spiritus,
> Et emitte coelitus
> Lucis tuae radium.

That humble invitation, and that acknowledgement of our human incompleteness, is the beginning of

CONCLUSION

the sequence through which the soul's transformation is accomplished.

Da perenne gaudium

is the end. Come, thou Holy ; pour out in our dim lives the steadfast radiance of the Living Perfect. Give the perennial joy of those whose separate action is lost in the eternal Act of God. Between these terms lies the whole rounded work of Spirit in and upon the plastic human soul.

Printed in Great Britain
by Amazon